Unleash Your Power

Kirsten Blakemore

Unleash Your Power

By Kirsten Blakemore

I0169989

Unleash Your Power

Kirsten Blakemore

Unleash Your Power

© 2025 Kirsten Blakemore

Published by Kirsten Blakemore

Unleash Your Power

Kirsten Blakemore

Table of Contents

Unleash Your Power

Kirsten Blakemore

Unleash Your Power

Women have settled long enough. Own Your Past, it's your story. Be empowered now. Three steps to create your life according to you!

Kirsten Blakemore

Edited by Sue Blakemore

Kirsten Blakemore

Acknowledgments

For me, writing a book is really a culmination of experiences, wisdom shared and role models who have walked the road ahead.

I have a few very good friends that I can process through painful experiences to gain meaning as well as truly celebrate the "wins". But those friends are so valuable to me. Without their support, love, patience and humor I would not have the forgiveness, strength and resilience I have today.

Wisdom comes in different forms. Some is as a result of giving yourself fully and being able to look back with a deeper understanding of the why. I have found that being a Mother of two has graced me with the understanding of what it means to love fully, to hurt fully and to give over fully, for the lives I have been so blessed to have in this life. But the cost to wisdom is high and is far from easy, or it wouldn't be wisdom. I am so grateful for my sons every day and I thank them for their daily doses of wisdom. Connor and Mason, I love you with all of my heart.

Finally, my role models. These are people who have demonstrated behaviors that have stuck with me that have been etched into who I am today. Every business leader, athletic coach, parent (and more) must know the impact they will have on another human being's life. It is a huge responsibility. Two role models stand out in my life. My Father who

Unleash Your Power

Kirsten Blakemore

struggled as a father, husband and businessman. My father was a SERE school instructor (survival, evasion, resistance and escape) in the mountains in Maine when I was young. Growing up we did not go to baseball games or museums with him, rather he would take us to the mountains, and we would "survive" the weekends in pretty dire weather. He could teach what few can, yet he could not cope with "normal" life. He drank and escaped until his life finally ended from the abuse. My father was a role model for me of what not to do. Whether he knew it or not, his life taught me so much about what I didn't want for mine. I love him and respect the lessons I learned from him.

My Mom was the rock of my home growing up. She was and is an example of never-ending grace and giving. To this day, her life is in service of others. Every rebellious stage (I think I only had one), every painful moment in my life, she was there for me. I have watched and experienced her love, patience and forgiveness all of my life. For this reason, I dedicate this book to her. Without her (English teacher experience and grammar) support and her ability to make me feel like "writing a book is no big deal, just do it" I would not have the book I do today. Mom, I love you with all of my heart and I thank you.

Introduction

There was a time in my life when I believed that if I worked hard enough, sacrificed enough, and proved myself enough, I would finally feel worthy. But the truth is, no amount of outside validation can give us the permission we've been waiting for. That permission must come from within.

I've stumbled, I've failed, I've doubted myself more times than I care to admit. I've also risen, loved deeply, and discovered a strength in myself I didn't know existed. What I've learned is this: every experience, even the painful ones, carries wisdom. And those lessons—sometimes hard-earned—are the very keys that allow us to unlock our power.

This book isn't about perfection, and it's not about living up to someone else's definition of success. It's about reclaiming the driver's seat of your life. It's about shifting from victim to creator, from silence to voice, from proving your worth to owning it fully.

Women have carried invisible weights for generations—expectations, biases, responsibilities that we didn't always choose. And yet, here we are, stronger, wiser, and more capable than we've ever been. This is our time. I wrote this book because I want you to know that you are not alone in your struggles or your dreams. You are not behind. You are not too late. And you are certainly not "not enough." You already have everything you need inside of you. What this book will do is help you uncover it, strengthen it, and unleash it.

Together, we'll walk through a process that has helped me and countless other women redefine our stories. You'll learn to define what you truly want, align your thoughts and actions with your vision, and design the life that reflects your authentic power.

I share my own lessons not because I have it all figured out, but because I believe in the beauty of honesty. Vulnerability is not weakness—it's courage in its purest form. My hope is that as you read, you'll see yourself in these stories and give yourself permission to rise.

The truth is, you don't have to wait any longer. The moment you choose yourself, your life begins to shift. And when women rise, we don't just change our own lives—we change the world.

So, let's begin.

Chapter 1: 3 Steps to Greatness

"Character cannot be developed in ease and quiet. Only through experience of trial and suffering can the soul be strengthened, ambition inspired, and success achieved." Helen Keller

As an Executive Coach, Facilitator, and Keynote Speaker, I work with a variety of different people, a recurring theme in conversations is that many women have worked in positions where they have had to constantly prove their worth. Is that you?

Do you feel the grind, day in and day out, of having to defend your value to others? Does it exhaust you? Do you feel a constant pull to take a vacation? Are you burned out? While at work, do you feel at times like you're fighting a ghost? Maybe your colleagues don't appear to value your efforts, but never tell you outright?

People hold beliefs about everyone with whom they work. If those beliefs are reinforced, they begin to form biases, which compound with the biases people bring with them (e.g., "Women aren't as powerful as men"— according to a CEO I met). Some biases propel you forward while others are a barrier to forward momentum. The battles vary based on where you are and for whom you work.

Pam worked for an organization whose leadership team consisted of clique of white males from a very similar background. She joined the company thinking she would make a difference in people's lives, that her previous employment made her a perfect fit for this new position. However, she found herself repeatedly excluded from projects, and when she asked for feedback to find out what was preventing her from being included, she rarely received any helpful insights. She had to make assumptions as to why she was being excluded, and those assumptions hurt. Eventually, she left the firm.

Upon her exit from the company, she shared that because she was a woman and did not share in their specific set of strong religious beliefs, she was excluded, which impacted her pay and her confidence, and she was tired of it. It eroded her self-worth until she was miserable and left. The bias was too influential, and the men on the team couldn't see how their bias was impacting Pam and others in a negative way.

Maybe you've been impacted by others' biases and tried to unsuccessfully to fight them. Maybe you questioned your own worth: "I'm not smart enough, old enough (yes, age can be correlated with experience), experienced enough, skilled enough, strong enough, or male enough." Throughout my coaching and consulting career working with women, I've come to realize these challenges are pervasive and not isolated to my own experience. And so, the search outside ourselves for validation—from events, people, and promotions—continues without perceptible improvement. Perhaps you thought, "If I could only have this job, or if people would see my worth, then I'd land the perfect role and fulfillment would be mine." I'm sorry to say, that mission is futile.

With all the factors outside our control, it's easy to feel like a victim of both people and circumstance. It took me years of experiences to learn that I'm actually in the driver's seat. No more do I think and act like a victim.

I've learned how to experience fulfillment. I've found that being a victim limits my ability to show up and express my voice. I'm now a massive equity champion, and I won't sit back and watch unfair behavior ensue, no matter to whom it's happening.

I've taken these lessons I've learned and created a simple three-step process that you can use in any situation where you feel stuck. These steps will help you assume the driver's seat of your life and ultimately experience fulfillment.

The time is ripe for upward movement. Women now have more opportunities to have a seat at the table when it wouldn't have been possible before. Companies are now strategically focused on diversity and inclusion, and more and more of them are touting health and wellness as a goal they want their employees to achieve. With this progressive direction, we're encouraged to attain work-life balance. We realize we can bear children, run a household, and have a dream job simultaneously. Women are searching to find their voice, and we're at a critical point in that journey—we have to find our voice, to let it be heard.

Although we've come a long way in business, we still have a ways to go. While there are laws in place to support women's rights, loopholes remain. Consider this story:

I was working with a company's executive team when the head of HR stopped me outside the conference room. She became very emotional, tearing up as she explained her battles with the CEO, who she felt failed to see her true value. Working in a male-dominated company and industry, she was constantly trying to prove her worth within the company—even within her own department—and she was exhausted.

How often do you feel you have to prove your worth as a wife, a mother, an employee, or a friend? Defending yourself and your value every day requires so much extra energy, doesn't it?

The head of HR I just described learned some tools to use to strengthen her position and her relationship with the CEO. Ultimately, she came to realize that her leader would not change, and she was empowered to know that every day she comes to work she has a choice to stay there or to leave. When it gets bad enough, she will leave.

The real problem comes when, over time, she begins to question her own value. Before all else, you have to believe in yourself because dwindling self-confidence limits our ability to see all our options and take appropriate action. The effects of the type of situation in which the head of HR found herself extend into all aspects of self-image. Discrediting our value is like a spider web that touches all facets of our life; it severely impacts our confidence, our self-worth, and our ability to escape the victim stranglehold.

Women have struggled to maintain leadership positions (whether head of household, leading a team or a company, or being an independent contributor), to honor our authenticity, and to earn the respect of those who work for us and with us. Now, though, we have the power to create the life we've always wanted. Many of us have faced challenges that may have slowed us down, even brought us to a halt, but this book is designed to lift you back up, to teach you how to give yourself permission to make your dream a reality.

Many of us focus on the "how": How will I reach my goals? How will I meet the right people to assist me? When we focus on the "how," we skip an essential part of the picture—the "why" and the "what." When we get crystal clear on what we want and why it's so important to us, the "how" starts to fall into place. Throughout this book, you'll answer critical questions that will help you move forward with your desired career, whether that's a successful housewife or a CEO—whatever life you choose.

Unleash Your Power

Kirsten Blakemore

The three steps to creating your desired outcome are Define, Align, Design.

Step 1: Define It

Determine: Who is in charge of your life? The premise is that you are the author, the director, and the main character in your life. All the other factors, experiences and people make up your environment.

Clarify: Describe your goals. Define all the parts of what want for your life, short term and long term. What will they look like, feel like, sound like?

Examine: Lead from your authentic self.

Inspect: What are you thinking relative to what you want? Are your thoughts in harmony with your dream?

Step 2: Align It

Inside Out: First, analyze your thoughts to assess their alignment with your goals.

Outside In: Look to your environment (which consist of people, situations in which you find yourself, obstacles) as an indicator of the alignment of your goals.

Balance: Strive for balance through self-awareness so that when obstacles arise, you're less likely to overreact.

Step 3: Design It

Courage: Disappointment and perceived failures are part of the path. Learn to correct your course.

Confidence: Fake it till you make it.

Consistency: Learn tools to follow through. Build in your accountability for your outcomes. Measure success. Watch for evidence and celebrate the wins!

In this book you'll expose yourself to the lessons as you read, you'll begin to digest the information and then apply it to yourself, and finally, you'll journal. At the end of each chapter, I've provided takeaways (feel free to add your own). Then the journaling questions will help you go deeper with the material. The sooner you take ownership for your future growth and apply the tools within the book, the faster you'll receive the outcomes you seek.

Here are the steps to follow:

Workbook at the end of each chapter:

Digest the information you just read.

Imagine possibilities.

Journal.

Continue to add to your vision board as you build more of your dream.

Take action.

As with any new routine, using this three-step process Define, Align and Design may feel robotic or uncomfortable at first, but the more you use this process, you'll discover it becomes second nature to you. Find opportunities to utilize the three steps throughout your day. Then you can apply it to anything, from very small arguments to your large goals that you've always wanted to accomplish. Stick with it.

As you likely know, you must do something repetitively if you want it to become a habit or if you want it to become your organic response to achieving the desired outcomes. Give yourself permission to slip, to fail, to move forward, and to be all that you are.

Accept the beauty in you that makes you unique to this world. Leave the world brighter because of your presence. The world will benefit from you Unleashing Your Power, your true You!

Follow the three-step process of Define, Align, Design for the small outcomes you want to accomplish as well as to pave the road to achieving your dreams.

Chapter 2: Define Your Goals

"Before assuming the driver's seat, one must find it."

Sue Blakemore

The first step in this process is to understand who's been driving your car. In dream therapy, the automobile represents you, so in the context of this metaphor, do you feel like you're in control of your life? Or do you feel buffeted about by others' choices and circumstances? Of course, the decision makers could be your boss, your co-workers, your friends, or your loved ones. To whom do you give decision-making authority? Throughout this chapter, we'll consider the possibility that you feel as though you have stumbled into the life you are currently living and want more for yourself. Furthermore, we will propose that you can create the life you choose moving forward!

The premise of this chapter is this: Define yourself or others will define you.

You need to own your past, create your present, and shape your future. Consider that for a moment: if you had the ability to create your life, how empowering would that be? Does that question bring to mind experiences where your felt out of control? Do you feel like exclaiming, "I didn't create that!"? If you stick with this idea that you DID create that, though, what did you (or could you) learn from the experience? Taking back control over

Kirsten Blakemore

your life requires tremendous self-reflection, which enables you to WAKE UP YOUR LIFE and make conscious choices moving forward.

Maybe you can relate to this story:

My client Laura prided herself on the standards of practice she'd developed over years of work. She drove herself to produce the highest level of work in everything she did, setting a very high bar for herself, both at work and at home where she ran the household. Her efforts were so tireless that she naturally drew attention to herself and was offered a high-paying position that would demonstrate her value and allow her to shine. Unfortunately, it didn't work out that way. She didn't accomplish what she claimed she would. She began to feel like a victim of her circumstances and believed she was alone without help. She spiraled down into helplessness and eventually was asked to leave the job. Her perfectionism ideal that she'd worked years to create was shattered.

Control versus Choice

In every situation, you have a choice. You may not be able to control your environment or the people around you, but you do control yourself with your attitude and how you show up. How you respond and react in all situations is your choice. After much reflection, Laura began to realize she had choices she'd overlooked; her need to control her situation had clouded her ability to see that.

Unleash Your Power

Kirsten Blakemore

Have you ever felt the need to control someone or something because you feared what could happen? If you answered "yes" to that question, that suggests you're trying to control someone or something because you think that if you don't, they won't act the way you want them to or the situation will turn out differently than how you'd like.

Someone dear to me is in a relationship in which the woman is trying to change the man, exclaiming that all the problems in their marriage rest on his shoulders. If he would just change, they'd be fine. However, it doesn't work like that, as I told her. We have to 100 percent own our choices in relationships. We can't control other people, no matter how much we'd like to. What we can do, though, is choose the best course of action based on what we perceive. We can control ourselves.

Problem versus Solution

I work with many people in businesses who have struggled with feelings of being overwhelmed and stuck. They feel fatigued, helpless, and without a choice as to how they show up, but they continue to look at all the problems they're facing that continue to keep them stuck. This thinking can take you on a tornadic downward spiral that decimates anything in its path. Time and again I hear that leaders (including CEOs) are the problem, and if we could just fix them, then all our problems would be solved. Regardless of whether the top echelon of your corporation lacks good management qualities, focus on your response. You can't control them, but you can control your own thinking and how you respond.

Adopt this mindset: "I know the solution is out there. I may not know what it is yet, but I'll keep looking until I figure it out." When we feel out of control, we focus on the problems in our lives. When we feel we're in a situation where we have a choice, we look toward the solutions. It's a mindset we choose.

Mindful Moment

For a Mindful Moment, imagine you're in a situation in which you feel like you have no control. How does that feel? Be aware of any physical reactions you're having. Remain in that moment until you're fully aware of the experience of being "out of control."

Now, do the same practice, but this time imagine you have choices and you're directing the outcomes. Does that resonate physically in your body? Be fully present with this experience, feeling the emotions, the physical sensations, and where your mind may be.

This is a Mindful Moment, a tool you can use anytime. I encourage you to use these Mindful Moments in your life to draw on your own personal awareness.

Consider the last time you weren't happy in a situation and you looked for more reasons to bolster your position. You wound yourself up and felt so

Kirsten Blakemore

justified in feeling that way. You may have even sought out people who would support your pity party, which just exacerbated the whole situation and left you feeling even more stuck.

We've all been there. One group with whom I was working told me their new moto was, "You can visit Pity City, just don't move in."

Below are some examples of mindsets that hold you back and some that will propel you forward. The key is to be aware of your mindset. Maybe you've created more than what I've listed below. Beautiful! The point is that you need to be aware of what you're thinking because it will drive what comes next.

Traps and Triumphs

These are mindsets that prevent positive outcomes. Three stoppers to avoid:

The Self-Doubter: This is the inner critic in your head that tells you, "It will never work," "You aren't good enough," or some version of that.

The Excuse Maker: This one comes up with reasons why you shouldn't do or why you should delay doing _____ (fill in the blank).

The Perfectionist: This one is cunning. It tells you that what you do and what you think are never good enough. You'll never reach perfection, so disappointment will always loom around the corner.

The flip side are the Catapulters that can bring you closer to your goals:

Unleash Your Power

Kirsten Blakemore

The Adventurer: You're always willing to try new approaches and activities.

The Visionary: You're able to see the potential in every situation.

The Go-Getter: No matter what, you'll go forward with hope and faith that there's something to be achieved.

Only you can create the life you want. Even though outside events—from the unexpected loss of a loved one to the damage caused by a hurricane—can seem to rob you of full control over your life, only you can determine what happens next. Instead of letting a calamity derail your dreams, use the experience to drive you forward with even more courage and determination.

If you refrain from labeling an experience as good or bad and simply learn from it, you won't empower it with negativity; you'll simply learn from it. Giving power to the negative experience fosters more negativity and additional similar events. (We'll discuss this in further detail in the Align section because of its importance.)

There's no denying that challenges, obstacles, and change are part of living life. For instance, I was speaking to a woman with whom I work and respect, and we were discussing the elements of work that we don't appreciate at all (including people). As we talked, we uncovered why some of the experiences we've had bothered us, and the whole conversation seemed rather bleak.

Unleash Your Power

Kirsten Blakemore

As we were concluding our call, though, we openly discussed the negative discussion and how it left us feeling "judgy" and bad. I offered that sometimes it's important to process through what's bothered us and why we didn't feel good after those experiences. We uncovered what we didn't like and value, which directed us into a discussion of what we really did like and desired for the future.

We took the conversation in a positive direction, discussing what we want in the future that will make us feel awesome! We both left the conversation really clear about what our own next steps were as we moved to creating what we want in our careers.

Take a moment to consider a time you had a job you loathed (maybe that's now). It uncovered the aspects you don't want in a job, didn't it? Unfortunately, that's where so many put their focus—on the unwanted elements. Instead, you need to reframe what you've learned into a positive statement of what you do want.

When you're reading a novel, you expect the main character to encounter obstacles that get in the way of the desired goal, and in a book, that goal is fairly clear. In life, however, it can be rather murky. Although we anticipate obstacles will arise in a story, we're often surprised when they occur in our life, and we fall victim to these circumstances quickly. Giving into thoughts such as, "There's nothing I can do about that. I guess I have to give up," can make the goal twice as unlikely to be achieved. An important question we need to ask ourselves is "In this situation, what can I control?"

If you can accept and embrace the contrast that surrounds us and that the unwanted will be there along with the wanted, then you'll be more flexible when tough situations arise. We have to understand what's good and bad in each situation in order to truly appreciate what we want or wish to avoid. You cannot create your life and be a victim to it. The empowered mindset is the premise that you create your future with your thoughts, attitude, and behavior. We've all encountered situations where we find ourselves asking "Why did that happen?" Maybe it's only in retrospect that you truly can see how your actions dictated the end result; maybe it wasn't your actions or inaction, but your attitude was unhelpful. If you find yourself saying something like, "This will never work," it likely won't.

You've probably heard the saying, "Find something for which you can be grateful." There's merit to that. When we look for areas in our life for which we're grateful, we're shaping our attitude. The more evidence we see of good around us, the more we continue to find. It's a looping process, and it reinforces what we want and actively shapes a positive, grateful frame of mind. When we have a positive attitude, we make better choices. We no longer see ourselves as a victim but as a designer of our own life instead.

Unleash Your Power

Kirsten Blakemore

To make this clearer, think about people who are so negative you avoid them. Have you ever been to a meeting where individuals are complaining and blaming? It creates a negative feeling, doesn't it? (Have you even been that person?) The proximity of negative people weighs you down, and their negativity is infectious. When the mind is rampant with negativity, we lose the ability to see clearly. In fact, if you have a negative disposition at the moment, you may be looking for someone to reinforce that, but how does that end? Maybe you feel good temporarily, but you don't get any closer to the positive outcome you want.

Like attracts like. The only way you can begin to attract positives in your life is to switch the dial on your attitude to positive. As I tell my kids, have an attitude of gratitude, a mindset that is so important I'll reiterate it throughout the book. If you focus solely on the negative, on finding negative events, people, and experiences to justify your position, then that's where you'll stay. Even if positive events occur in your life, if you have a negative mindset, you'll miss them.

A word of caution: don't fall into the victim mentality. When I work with individuals and teams, I often hear people say, "If they'd change, everything would work," or "If they'd just get their act together, I could do my job." Let's personalize that: "If people would just stop misunderstanding me, I could get _____ (fill in the blank: a mate, a better relationship, a

Kirsten Blakemore

promotion)." When you make these types of statements, you put all the control and choice outside yourself. It's is a victim mentality.

Here's what it sounds like when you're not a victim: "Boy, I feel really misunderstood. What am I saying or doing that's causing this outcome?" See the difference? The first statement is from a victim perspective; the second statement is from an empowered perspective. You choose which perspective you want to operate from. You always have a choice.

Although there will always be elements in your life you can't control, you can control you. How do you choose to show up in a situation that you felt was out of your control? Every choice you make defines your now and creates your future. We can swing on the pendulum from where we feel stuck to where we feel so fearful of the future we try to control everything on our path. Ideally, though, we'd choose the middle where we have a sense of, "I control me, and I positively influence what's around me." This mindset will likely give us the greatest sense of peace.

However, if we're somewhere near either end of the pendulum arc, we'll likely feel defeated. At one end of the arc, we'd have a feeling of no control, and being stuck at the other end of the arc would make us feel very uptight and angry as we try to control everything. Sadly, when we try to control everything and everyone else but ourselves, we can't feel a sense of empowerment or peace. When we feel empowered with choice and in

Unleash Your Power

Kirsten Blakemore

control of our destiny, we make space to create the future we desire, and we can be present with those we love.

Look at the illustration below. Where do you fall in your current situation?

Attitude of Gratitude

This is a moment-by-moment process and recognizing that we choose our attitude is the next step to creating change. Find opportunities to bolster and shape a grateful, positive attitude.

Once we can acknowledge our response or reaction in any given situation, we can begin to actively choose how we want to show up, and this choice is what determines the life we create. There's a difference between trying to control life and trying to create the life you want. I see many women and leaders try to control their people and their surroundings and the change that always comes. The problem with this is the motivation for their actions. The genesis of control is fear. The misconception is that if you control your life, then you leave less to chance and uncertainty; life is uncertain though, and change is always present. As a leader, a mother, and a woman, we need an element of trust—trust that your people will deliver, your life will turn out well, and that change is for the better.

I'm not saying sit back and watch. You must be an active creator in your life, but again the difference is motivation. Are you coming from a place of fear? Are you trying to control others? Or are you coming from a place of trust? Are you actively defining and pursuing the life you want? Do you support the people who work for and with you?

Reflections:

Takeaway: Create your own life.

Choose your attitude, thoughts, and behavior.

Understand that like attracts like.

Practice self-reflection.

List some of your own takeaways:

Journal: Where is the resistance that stops me from assuming full choice of my life?

Where do I feel I'm a victim to my circumstances?

Who in my life provokes me to feel I have no choice?

If I were to take one idea from this chapter and incorporate that into my life, which one would that be and why?

Chapter 3: Define & Clarify the Details

"The best way to predict the future is to create it." Abraham Lincoln

Defining what you want is the first, most important step, yet it's the one least likely to happen. Life tends to move ahead at warp speed (especially if you have children), and most of us spend much of our day on autopilot, moving from one task to the next. You may be like me, juggling work with preparing meals, interacting with my kids, and chauffeuring them to all their activities. Whatever stage of life you inhabit, your tasks may be different, but you'll still have daily demands. Now is the time to ask yourself what you really want (besides peace and quiet).

Define the life you want to create for yourself. If you don't clarify what you want your life to be, you may not be thrilled with the results. As I go through this process with my clients, they focus first on defining what they do not want, which may be a natural place for us to turn. But as I guide my clients in the direction of what they do want, the dialogue changes and they are much more energized with the outcomes.

Contrast Creates Clarity

How much time do you invest in exactly what you want versus what you don't want? When you catch yourself saying, "I don't like my manager" or "I don't want …," you fall into the mind trap. This is the opposite of what we need to do, and yet our environment trains us to dwell on the negative.

Unleash Your Power

Kirsten Blakemore

In and of itself, the negative isn't bad because the contrast it provides gives us a clear picture of what we don't want. So once we determine what we don't want—the contrast—we need to consider what we do want. In order to create the life we want, we must consider our thoughts, feelings, and actions because those determine our life.

Your Why

Mark Twain said, "The two most important days in your life are the day you are born and the day you find out why."

Living our why fulfills us.

Given that premise, what do you see in your future? As you explore in detail what it is you want, the next step will be to focus attention on that because we create what claims our focus. The why is critical to this process. Have you spent time considering what your purpose is—why you're here and what you have to offer that's unique to you? Many times there's a strong correlation between the why you want something and your purpose.

What inspires your passion?

Is there anything at work that really excites you? For some, it's the relationships we form at work that keep us engaged and eager to succeed. For others, a good leader has gained our loyalty. Still others know that having a strong cause is one way to increase engagement at work.

Unleash Your Power

If you haven't ever thought about your purpose, or if you haven't been able to figure it out, consider what wakes you up in the morning and makes you eager to jump into the day. When we feel engaged and passionate about what we're doing, we're fulfilled. Certainly, there will be bumps in the road, but overall we feel good about the work we're doing.

I met Robin Cartagena, a very close friend years ago at work. At that time, she was a superstar in the role she had. Although we no longer work together, we remain close. She's now a mother of three, one of which has special needs. Her job is head of household, and her desire to be the best mother and wife she can be is what drives her. She's one of the most passionate, fulfilled people I know, and she has a very clear idea about her purpose. Her energy for life is endless.

What energizes you? Is it a specific job? A project or a company? Or is it simply to be a great mom? Whatever your dream may be, start by creating a list of what you want the most, then begin adding details to your list. If you're searching for the perfect job, write down some details that would make it perfect.

As I mentioned before, when you start jotting down what you want in a job, you may find that it's easier to jot down what you don't want. Even though you're focusing on the dream job and its attributes, your mind may wander to what you don't want. Use the contrast to help you identify and specify what you do want. When you journal, though, write about those attributes that are attractive to you, the ones you desire.

For example, do you want a job that requires you to travel, or would you prefer to stay in an office with co-workers surrounding you all day? Do you prefer working remotely? Do you want to own your own business or do you prefer to have a consistent salary as an employee? Do you want to work for a large organization or a start-up? Are you energized considering working for non-profit or for-profit company? Be as specific as possible. Now, tie your emotions to it. If you were to land that job with all the specifics you listed, how would it make you feel and why? Be extremely detailed here. The why is really important.

Why do you want to lead a family within which you have mutual respect and a hefty balance of fun? Why do you want the job that will allow you to travel the world? Why would that be fulfilling? What would it do for you if you had that job?

The root of the why begins to address the source of your fulfillment, which is the indicator that we're doing what we love—or not. There's no magic in this process, but if you complete the steps in this book and are true to your inner compass, you'll find fulfillment.

Consider the dictionary definition of fulfillment: the achievement of something desired, promised or predicted. If you want to be fulfilled, the

Kirsten Blakemore

first step is to clearly define what that means for you so that you can create a fulfilling future.

The How

Journaling is a great way to foster more ideas about what it is you want, and ideally you should journal every day. It doesn't have to be much. Perhaps only a few sentences will add additional context and detail around what you're trying to achieve.

Although there are scientific, neurobiological reasons for free writing, let's skip that part and turn to where the rubber meets the road: If you dream it; write it; and consistently follow through with the right thoughts, feelings, and actions, it will come. It may not arrive tomorrow morning on your doorstep, but if you have faith and regularly put effort into your goals, you'll achieve them. Continue to gather your thoughts and experience the feelings you'll have when the dreams you wish to produce are already here. (This is where daydreaming is okay.)

In my struggle to find my perfect job, I journaled, providing detail around my perfect job and creating a dream (vision) board to reflect that. Part of my criteria was that this job would find me in less than sixty days. I had no idea what kind of jobs were out there in an industry with which I was unfamiliar, but I knew what I wanted to do and described it with specificity. During this time, I looked for opportunities and continuously took action.

Kirsten Blakemore

Visualization and journaling are important. Equally important, though, was the research I did to find jobs that contained those components on my dream list. Visualization, journaling, and action go hand in hand.

In less than sixty days I landed the perfect job. It was everything I'd written down in my journal—which I didn't even realize until I picked up the journal almost a year later. As I read my description of the "perfect job," I realized I was in it. I'd found it! Not only did this reinforce my approach, but it increased my confidence that I could actually accomplish this! Let me tell you, this works!

Visualize, journal, and search for opportunities to take action. The journaling provides you with a reference, a historical snapshot. As you master this fluid process, refer back to what you wrote previously to learn what changes you may require. You can use this vision boarding process for a dream job, a new relationship, or any other goal you hope to achieve.

If you could create your future, what would you do? What elements would you include in this perfect situation? Be crystal clear when you describe what you want, and don't jump ahead until this is complete.

Once the clarity is in place, the next step is how. How do I get there? Keep your eyes open for opportunities to ask for help (one might call this research). For example, when I decided I wanted to write a book, I had to consider who to ask for help. I had to find out what the first step should be.

Unleash Your Power

Kirsten Blakemore

These inquiries and/or online research should provide fuel for you to continue on the path toward achieving it.

It's normal to experience fear during a process like this, so don't let it stop you or hold you back. When you decide you want to do something new, crazy, or outside the area that you think you could achieve, fear (the stalker) will enter the picture. Go into this knowing fear will be there but keep moving forward anyway. Surround yourself with ideas and people who will support your dream and remember that this process starts with your thoughts. Think about what you want, then attach the why to it because the why arouses your emotions, which will lead to the how and the what. Look for opportunities to take action.

Example of Vision Board:

This is my friend's vision board that she built for her dream job in service of others.

Reflection:

Takeaway: We create our own life with our thoughts, feelings, and actions.

Clarify in detail what you want and include the passionate why.

Elucidate what fuels your passion.

Look for opportunities to take action.

List some of your own takeaways

Unleash Your Power

Kirsten Blakemore

Journal: What is my purpose? My why?

What are my short-term and long-term goals?

What is my perfect job, or what is my idea of a perfect relationship?

Why do I want those things? (In other words, if I had this, would I jump

out of bed each day, eager to start?)

What actions can I take that will bring me closer to my dream?

Chapter 4: Examine: Lead from Your Authentic Self

"To be yourself in a world that is constantly trying to make you something else is the greatest accomplishment."

Ralph Waldo Emerson

Over the years I've asked many women in executive roles to what they attribute their success. I lead from my authentic self, is the predominant answer.

I believe that leading from our authentic self requires us to follow our inner moral compass. Following the inner moral compass may neither be easy nor popular. If there seems to be a right and a wrong, I need to choose right. This is powerful. Some of the toughest decisions we face require us to choose a path at the fork in the road. One path may lead to short-term power that requires us to bring others down in order to elevate our status or position. Another path could be to stay silent while witnessing an employee throw another co-worker under the bus. While the path might feel shaky, you know in your gut it's the right choice. When you choose this, it reinforces the decisiveness, bravery, and power you have within you. We know when we've listened to our gut and when we've ignored it. Here are some examples clients have shared with me:

Unleash Your Power

Kirsten Blakemore

I was interviewing people for a position that would report to me. I found candidates that could "do the job," but I found one who was amazing. I was afraid that amazing person would make me look bad and even, worst-case scenario, take my job, so I ended up hiring one of the people that could just "do" the job.

I was in a meeting with our president who asked about a project and why it was not complete. I told him that it was the marketing manager's fault for not getting it done. I pointed the finger. I could have chosen to share some of the roadblocks which confronted us, and how it was nothing short of amazing that the project was still as far along as it was. Instead, I just threw my colleague under the bus so I would look good to the president. Technically, I didn't do anything wrong … but my gut felt like I was sucker-punched.

I was interviewing for a new position within my company and I knew others were vying for it too. I was asked questions that put me in a position of having to choose to elevate myself by pulling others down and I fell for it. I put my colleagues down so I would look good but felt awful when I left the interview.

I shared vital information with my colleague that was critical to the success and new direction the organization wanted to take. Unbeknownst to me, my colleague took that information as his own to the acting CEO, resulting

Unleash Your Power

Kirsten Blakemore

in a promotion [for my colleague] and my termination. I left willingly without exposing my colleague who I thought was my friend.

We all face difficult choices like the examples I shared here. Do we want to lead an authentic life and choose the right path? Are we motivated and seduced by our fears to choose the path that requires us to be less than decent, less than honorable? Movies always depict the main character having to make a tough decision: lead an authentic, honest life or lead a life that's deceptive, greedy, and power hungry. We root for the character who chooses the honest choice.

Listen to Your Gut

Choices aren't always fun, easy, or clear, and making a choice often requires us to tune in to our gut. When I say "gut," I mean there's a higher power— one not attached to ego—inside each of us that's our guidance system. If we tune in, we can find the answers we seek. If we ignore it, we're left feeling less-than. When we make poor choices, we may start to justify why we had to do what we did, which can spiral down into negative self-talk, lack of confidence, and self-doubt.

Anger is a response that's an easy lever to pull when we want to control our environment, but if anger's the first floor, fear is the basement. Fear is a motivator for anger and negativity, and all together, fear, anger, and negativity repel and take us farther away from our moral compass. These

Kirsten Blakemore

emotional responses create barriers between us and others and are reactive not proactive. Leading authentically requires thought, introspection and self-awareness.

Live and lead from your authentic self; anything less is a façade. The problem of living a façade is that it takes energy to maintain it, and that depletes your value. Being true to yourself is empowering. When you're tuned in to your moral compass, it will be easier to make the right or fair decision.

Have you ever squelched a thought or comment because you didn't think it would be popular? Consider this: If we ignore or push down thoughts or feelings because we believe they won't be popular or appropriate, they'll fester and burst at some point. I call it a stack attack. All the little things we ignore, push down, justify, or squelch start to build until one little thing sets us off and we explode because we're not addressing something or not being true to ourselves. Now, this doesn't mean you should go shouting from the rooftops, exclaiming statements of your truth, but it does mean you should listen to your gut and honor it with grace.

To lead an authentic life, you must own every aspect of you. Are you hiding your voice to preserve an image you want to project?

Being authentic requires bravery. My dear friend gave me a bracelet I wear all the time that says, "be brave." It's my reminder in every situation that I must be brave, which usually requires me to take the tougher path. When women make the choice to be authentic, we become stronger leaders, stronger women. The more authentic you are, the more you condition yourself to decipher which decision is the right one in any given situation. For some, you may feel it in your gut. Others may sense it, or some may even hear it. Whatever it is for you, become good at listening to your inner wisdom in whatever form it takes. Listening to your inner voice of wisdom is a skill. By being true to yourself, your voice will be heard.

Mindful Moment:

Close your eyes and think back to a time when you had a tough decision to make. Maybe it was a choice in your relationship or at work. What were some thoughts you considered as you weighed your options? When did you know that was the choice you were going to make? How did it feel in your body, and where did you feel it? What did the feeling tell you? In retrospect, do you feel you made the right and fair decision, or were you simply trying to be right?

Reflection:

Takeaway: Our value has the greatest impact when we lead authentically.

Measure today's actions by your authenticity ruler. Is this really who I am and who I want to be?

Unleash Your Power

Kirsten Blakemore

Anger stems from fear and pulls you away from your inner moral compass.

Bravery is living authentically.

List some of your own takeaway's.

Journal: What does it mean for me to be authentic?

Where did I shine?

Where could I improve?

What does my inner wisdom/moral compass tell me is important?

Chapter 5: Inspect: My Strengths Are My Brand

"We delight in the beauty of the butterfly but rarely admit the changes it has gone through to achieve that beauty." Maya Angelou

Your Strengths

The three women standing in the hotel ballroom at their company meeting discussed how different they felt from their peers. They were consistently left out of projects because they were women but continued to discuss how they could do things differently. Cheryl, who had been with the firm the longest and was feeling defeated by the exclusive behavior of her male colleagues, suggested this wasn't normal. She added that she was feeling like maybe she didn't have the value the team needed. Her female friends pushed back on that notion and suggested this new norm wasn't due to their lack of value or strength. The women agreed with this but were angered by the flagrant bias. As they discussed their options, they didn't want to resort to anger and defeat.

Because the women hadn't experienced this level of exclusion with previous employers, it was taking a toll on their confidence and self-worth, so together the women began exchanging feedback with each other. They shared what they believed were the strengths of each woman present so that each would have that outside perspective. What had begun as a negative turned into a valuable discussion. Each woman left the conversation more confident in her worth and the value she brings to the job, regardless of the obvious exclusion.

Some of your experiences may have left you feeling undervalued, but it's important to remember that we're each born with unique gifts. As we grow, we experience areas in which we flourish and talents that expand. We find opportunities to do more of that which satisfies us, and when we do, we're in our element. If you're reading this and thinking that you may not have any unique talents, think again; perhaps this resonates with you, but you don't have time to focus on those unique qualities; or perhaps you have a quiet voice within you that says pursue them!

Use this section to identify your strengths. What are your specific talents that have been celebrated in the past? In what ways have you personalized those talents to make them uniquely yours? (Perhaps you have a good sense of humor. Do you use that to diffuse difficult situations?)

If you're not fully aware of and anchored in your own strengths, then you may look to others and see theirs. When that happens, you fall into the trap of wishing you were that person or you had that person's strengths, qualifications, experience, wisdom, body, and … on and on. It's easy to lose focus on what you have to offer and instead look outside yourself to what others have to offer. On the one hand, we can admire others' strengths to see how we can incorporate them into our own way of doing things. On the

Unleash Your Power

Kirsten Blakemore

other hand, we can fall into a trap and tell ourselves, "Clearly I'm not good enough because I don't have that characteristic." And what a seductive trap it can be.

When you fall into that mire, your negative mind takes a mud bath. Your inner critic finds all the reasons why another person is more qualified, educated, and just all around better to the point that you come to believe that clearly you're not good enough. Self-doubt is pervasive. When you fall into this trap, you can totally lose focus on your own worth and your strengths. Don't get caught in the quagmire of desperation and despair, and guard against adding a dose of perfectionism, which will complete the mud bath as well as thwart your ability to see clearly the path that lies ahead. Discipline is required to keep your focus on where you shine.

Maybe you have a difficult time discerning what makes you a unique, important member of society. One way to begin the process of identifying these traits in yourself is to ask for feedback from your peers, relatives, or subordinates. Ask them what they perceive to be your talents and take what they say and create a list: your sense of humor, your ability to remain calm in a storm, your tremendous attention to detail, your organizational skills, and so forth.

Those specific strengths that you (and others) have been identified form a brand, so the next step is to identify your brand. Are you the one to whom people turn for very creative solutions, or are you the one who knows how to foster relationships within a group?

Assess Your assets

If you struggle with identifying your strengths, you may find value in a third-party test, such as 360's, StrengthsFinder, and StandOut just to name a few. Not only will these tests reinforce what you may already know, they can also unveil new insights that you hadn't previously considered.

After taking the StandOut assessment test, I found that I'm in the line of work now (after twenty years of trying to find where my passion lies) that supports my strengths. These results were simply a reinforcement of what I experience when I'm living my dream. There's likely a correlation between your strengths and your purpose, so when you find your purpose and live it, you'll feel fulfilled. Below are the links to the StandOut Assessment and to StrengthsFinder.

As you continue to assess your assets, be honest about who you are, your skill set, and what you need to move forward. Never stop learning. One executive reported that she has a philosophy of lifelong learning. Another mentioned that she reads, studies, takes classes, and speaks with other leaders to stay current in her field. Like these successful women, always continue to grow, understanding that we're never a finished product. Your focus must be to continue to grow in ways that will support the areas in which you want to excel.

Ideally, you want to find an organization that supports employee development programs. Thankfully, so many companies understand the benefit of continuing to cultivate their people. I've spoken at many organizations where they have leadership certification programs. Their identified high performers are encouraged to complete classes, at the end of which they're certified. Take advantage of those programs your organization has to offer, and if you're currently seeking employment, ask during your interviews what development programs they have in place for employees, as well as if there is tuition reimbursement for graduate programs. Currently there are many opportunities to build your skills because companies understand having these programs in place builds their employee bench strength, making the companies more competitive in the marketplace.

Once you've defined the life you want, the company where you want to work, and the role you want to take, you can start to identify areas you need to develop to be competitive, always keeping your eyes open for opportunities. It's easy to fall into the trap where women can become mired: "Well, if I only had this skill, I could interview for that job," or "If I had this experience, I'd definitely put my name in the hat, but because I don't, I won't," or "I don't have time." Make the time—you're worth it!

Men are much more likely to interview for a job for which they have little experience. It seems our society has engendered more confidence in men in general than in women. That's the differentiator. As you've probably often heard, "Fake it till you make it." Many times a great attitude and a zest for the challenge will win over experience to give you a seat at the table.

Reflection:

Takeaway:

My strengths are my brand.

Those with whom I work are a resource for feedback.

I can take a strengths-based test for third-party validation.

Needing to be perfect holds me back from living life (and may also endanger the lives of others).

List any other takeaway for yourself.

Journaling:

What do I love to do?

What are my strengths?

How will I identify them? From whom will I ask for feedback?

Can I be honest with myself and accept my strengths?

In what areas do I refrain from participating because I think I may be "not good enough"?

Unleash Your Power

Kirsten Blakemore

What skills do I need to develop or enhance, what books do I need to read,

or what courses do I need to take to help me attain the position I want?

Chapter 6: Align with Self-Analysis

"We must not allow other people's limited perceptions to define us."

Virginia Satir

Align Your Thoughts

This section is about ensuring that your thoughts, feelings, and actions are aligned with what you want. The perceptions that others hold about you must work for you and not against you.

Typically, we don't realize that our thoughts aren't supporting our goals. Only in retrospect do we become aware of the self-doubt that plagued our forward movement. So many women in impressive roles have shared that this alone was their biggest obstacle to overcome. Ensuring that our thoughts aren't ambushing our goals is the hardest—but most critical—step to our success.

When I surveyed women in executive positions in very large organizations, they attributed success to responding with a positive attitude when things didn't go their way. Many had received promotions and awards when other candidates were equally qualified. They asked, "Why me?" and were told that their positive attitude that separated them from the others. That has influenced me ever since; after all, our thoughts and feelings are interrelated.

Unleash Your Power

Kirsten Blakemore

Do any of these following questions sound familiar? How am I ever going to finish the project on time? I'll never get this promotion—why am I even trying to interview for it? It's clear my boss favors my colleague. I'll never be able to compete with them. I have so many competing priorities, and my plate's already full. I don't even know where to start.

If those are (or were) your thoughts, imagine what feelings would result from them—defeat, depression, discouragement … Those feelings foster additional, similar thoughts, which in turn produce the same kind of feelings. This is what we label a downward spiral. Typically, those thoughts lead to further negativity, which thwarts confidence, courage, and clarity because our mind is mired in the swamp of self-doubt.

Sequentially, thoughts produce feelings, which produce more thoughts, which ultimately lead to action or inaction. Those actions we take (or our inaction) will be determined by the thoughts and feelings we previously had and are based on our ongoing, internal dialogue, determining how productive (or not) we are. People around us, of course, are not privy to our internal dialogue, but they see our actions. Are your resulting actions helping you achieve your goals?

Take Control

This is where you turn to self-analysis. Where are your thoughts turning to doubts? Are those thoughts in line with what you want to achieve? If you allowed yourself to be a director in your internal dialogue, what would you like the script to say?

The first step is recognizing the dialogue when self-doubt creeps in because the faster you recognize it, the faster you'll regain the director's chair. Take control of those negative thoughts and make a choice. Do you want to stay negative, or are you ready to change the story and become (at least) optimistic?

I'm going to share with you some tools you can use to recognize and change the dialogue.

One method is to wear a rubber band on your wrist. When the voice of self-doubt speaks up, snap the rubber band to change the narrative. Just as we give a child a time out to reconsider their choices, you can give yourself a time out when the story turns ugly.

Humor, another tool, always removes the seriousness of the situation. Early on in my career, I worked with a group of people I would call friends. Our meetings with the President always ended with him yelling at one of us. It was so stressful because we never knew who had the bullseye on their head during that meeting. We would try to make light of those meetings by suggesting we sing during the meeting to derail the yelling. We would all end up laughing at the thought of it. It would deflate the anxiety we all felt walking into the meeting.

Unleash Your Power

Kirsten Blakemore

Another method you can utilize when the situation turns dire is stop, drop, and roll. When a negative story is happening in your head, STOP. Recognize that it's a negative narrative and stop it. Next, DROP this story and reframe it until it's at least neutral, but better yet positive. Finally, ROLL with your new positive version.

For example, your boss gives a directive to you and the team. The narrative in your head quickly becomes something like this: The directive must be a result of my failure. The last time we had to do this project, the approach was different. He must have modified it to dummy-proof it because of me. Using this method, STOP to recognize you're creating a potentially damaging story based on your fear of inadequacy. Consider that you don't know why the directive was given. Reframe it in your mind and decide that his instruction will benefit the outcome of the project and may even be a result of some comments you made. DROP the old, damaging narrative and replace it with the new one without assumptions. ROLL with the new story. When you're creating the new narrative, it's not wrong to double-check with the person to see if there are any beliefs working against you of which you should be aware.

Reframing your thoughts enables them to line up with what you want to achieve, but this requires discipline and awareness. Imagine in detail what you want to create as a perfect future. If your thoughts and actions aren't aligned with that vision, it won't happen.

Mind Your Mind

So, just to reinforce what we've covered so far, the first step is to have the vision, and the second is to align your thoughts so that they harmonize with your dream. Are your thoughts supporting your efforts? Likely, because you're human, you have times when they support you and times when they don't, but what's the split? If you were to estimate the percentage of the day that your negative thoughts prevailed, what would that number be? If you don't know, keep track for a day by placing a tick mark (indicating negative thinking) on a white board or sticky pad. If you find you've only slipped once or twice, good going! If you have several check marks, however, consider the events that occurred that provoked your negative thinking and be aware of where your mind is.

Keep track of your negative thoughts in this manner for a week. Can you recall what occasioned your negative thinking? What did the negative talk in your head tell you? Did it hold you back? Did it prevent you from action? If so, it might be because of a survival mechanism built into us, a voice that suggests we should be afraid and not go into battle. It's our fight-or-flight response.

Unleash Your Power

Kirsten Blakemore

In the coaching world we refer to the negative voice as a gremlin or a saboteur, or some simply give it a name of its own, arguing that naming your negative voice can make it less invasive and unruly. Whatever the name, it's that voice in your head that tells you that you're not good enough; that you're not experienced enough, thin enough, rich enough, pretty enough … you get the point—enough already! It's the voice that tries to derail you when what you really need is a voice of support and encouragement.

One circumstance that really evokes this negative talk is when change is afoot—and when is it not? Successful women have told me over and over that they've embraced change instead of resisting it. Change is one of life's sureties: change will happen. How will you greet it? Will you resist it or fight it? Or will you welcome it as an opportunity to learn and grow?

None of us like this negative, doubting voice in our head that attempts to hold us back. The key is to acknowledge it and change the story. Although that's easier said than done, here are some tips to help change your story.

1. Begin to recognize when that gremlin is speaking to you and filling your mind with self-doubt.

2. Take an outside position and listen to what it's telling you. (For example, it may tell you, You won't do well in that job interview. You're not good enough. Or maybe it will say, You're not good enough to compete. Listen

as if you were dealing with a child because we're likely to be much more compassionate with a child than we are with ourselves. Ask the thought, What are you trying to tell me? Is it a message to protect me? Is it a message to hold me back from the unknown because that space is too scary? What would my situation need to look like for me to feel safe?

3. You can even give the process a name like HAL. HAL: Hear it, Acknowledge it, Let it go. It becomes less real and stifling when you walk through that process.

Coping Mechanism Personas - Reactors

When we encounter any kind of stress or an obstacle arises, we resort to coping mechanisms, which we often learn in childhood to handle environmental situations. They taught us how to navigate through each event. Although our coping mechanisms may have been helpful when we were kids, some of them may not be as effective or useful now that we're adults. They may even work against us. I've encountered seven typical coping mechanism types in business, although there may be more.

Victim

Blamer

Disengager

Passive-Aggressor

Procrastinator

Kirsten Blakemore

Negative Naysayer

Lecturer

The victim coping mechanism is designed to keep the world outside by positioning ourselves as helpless to other people or to circumstances. It keeps us stuck where we are and limits how we view the world. The call of the victim sounds like this: I can't do anything because of these things that are outside my control, or I'm trapped without options in this job that I hate.

The blamer goes a step farther and assigns fault to other people, places, and things and lacks ownership. One researcher states that blame is the way we discharge our discomfort with our current internal environment. This may intrude in a variety of ways, for example: (1) If I had a better boss, I could do my job more effectively, (2) If my co-workers were more organized, I could get my project competed on time, or (3) My team is disorganized, so I have to do their jobs and mine; of course I can't get it done in time.

The disengager coping mechanism keeps life at bay. We detach from our emotions because we don't care about the outcome (nor do we feel like we can impact the outcome). We feel our voice isn't heard anyway, so why bother speaking up and staying engaged? We've checked out!

The passive-aggressor wants to be liked and thus will be the "yes" person, the one who needs other people's approval. But an internal battle ensues, and they resent the position in which they find themselves and will backhand a person, place, or thing. You'll notice this when a co-worker says, Yes, yes I'll do it, and then doesn't and doesn't follow up. There's just silence. (It's easier to recognize this in another person than in ourselves …) The procrastinator resorts to inaction as a way of controlling the situation. It's safer not to engage in the activity than to engage with potential unknown results. Uncertainty isn't a friend. These are the people who commonly miss timelines or are scrambling last minute to complete a project, resulting in less than top-quality work. You can't count on them.

The negative naysayer prevents change by discounting any potential, new idea. Typically, this coping mechanism uses negativity to thwart change efforts because change is scary and uncertain. Fear drives the negativity.

The lecturer tells everyone what to do or what they should do. She prides herself on knowing everything and confidently shares that with everyone; however, she seldom listens to anyone else's opinion.

These coping mechanisms are useful when it comes to keeping change in check, for ensuring status quo is our normal. You may find this list helpful as you begin to look at your most frequently used coping mechanisms. Do any of these prevent you from operating courageously and with excitement when facing change? If you find it difficult to identify your coping mechanisms, you may require a good friend or coach to help you identify yours. Eliminating less-than-helpful coping mechanisms leads to courageous, more joyful experiences in life. In essence, you're acknowledging and taking control of fear.

Our thoughts and feelings drive us closer to our goals or the move us farther away, making it impossible to achieve them. This is the Align step. Aligning your thoughts, feelings, and actions will move you toward your dreams, goals, desires, and RESULTS! This is empowering because ultimately, you're directing your life.

Reflection:

Takeaway:

Recognize if your thoughts are in line with your goals.

You can't reach your destination with your foot on the brake.

Align your thoughts with what you want to achieve.

Utilize tools to recognize and stop the negative chatter: Stop, Drop, and Roll.

Notice the voice of the inner critic and take an outside position, HAL.

Inventory yourself to see which of the seven coping mechanisms/reactors you use.

Journaling:

How often is my negative chatter present?

When does the gremlin typically rear its head?

Unleash Your Power

Kirsten Blakemore

Which coping mechanism is my favorite (hint: it's the one I use most frequently)?

Chapter 7: Align Outside In

"Our deepest fear is not that we are inadequate. Our deepest fear is that we are powerful beyond measure. It is our light, not our darkness that most frightens us. We ask ourselves, 'Who am I to be brilliant, gorgeous, talented, fabulous?' Actually, who are you not to be? You are a child of God. Your playing small does not serve the world." Marianne Williamson

I was in a meeting where I was proposing a new business idea. When I left the room, two people remained, and I noticed they closed the door after me and stayed for a bit. My mind started racing with self-doubt and the potential conversations they were having.

How often does your mind start racing with all the possibilities, which are usually negative? You can spin yourself into a space not helpful to you or your goals. Perhaps, you'll see yourself move into one of the Reactor Personas.

I waited for my emotions to stop swirling before I headed back into the office where one of the colleagues was sitting behind his desk.

"I noticed you both closed the door when I left," I said simply, "and my sense is there was a 'meeting after the meeting.' I want to know if you have any feedback for me on the meeting we just held?"

Kirsten Blakemore

We ended up having a good conversation, and I left with a concrete direction for my next steps. Had I not asked the question, I could still be pondering the many different dramatic scenarios I'd concocted in my head. This is the essence of Outside In. What people or events in your environment can influence your current thinking and outlook? Are your thoughts taking you in the direction of where your goals will mesh? How can you use those thoughts as indicators to help inform you of the direction you're headed?

One executive I spoke to described an experience she had with a colleague who she later found out was speaking poorly of her at every turn. That person left the company, and six months later she was promoted. She strongly believes the reason she was held at a standstill was this person's bad-mouthing, and when that person was gone, her path was clear for the promotion.

Are there people and experiences holding you back? Why are they, and what can you do to change it, to be in charge of you? What are your intentions? Are they positive, or are you being manipulative—or worse, deceitful? This chapter is about learning how to recognize what's happening inside you by looking at the people and experiences around you as indicators.

Uncovering Obstacles

Unleash Your Power

Kirsten Blakemore

One way to uncover the way people see you is to consider the situations at work. Do you feel included or excluded? Years ago, when I worked for a company and had just had my second child, I felt very excluded from the cliques that were composed of young, single people (or partnered people without families) who would grab drinks after work. I, on the other hand, would race out to pick up kids, grocery shop, cook, and clean until the next day when I'd sit in meetings and feel as though I'd missed conversations … because I had—at the bar the night before. Knowing what I know now, I could have conversed with one of them to find out what they'd discussed, what I missed. That would have made me look interested, and I would have learned more about what was discussed that was pertinent to my job.

Look around you to see some of the beliefs people may hold about you that are stalling your forward momentum. Use your environment to discover the lens through which people view you.

I was working with a team of leaders once who stated that one of their gaps was effective communication with another division upon which they relied to execute and deliver their service. This team was very clear that they were good communicators and the other people were the problem. "If they could just get their act together, then things would be good," they told me. When faced with the question, "What can you do to improve the situation?" they said they'd tried everything, and this group really was at fault. This leadership team felt stuck, as though they were victims of this situation—so much so that some in the group were trying to hold back tears. They just couldn't see that they had a choice in this situation.

How often have you felt stuck in a situation or with a person, like a manager (or maybe a husband or wife)? You felt as though you'd tried everything, yet the problem continued to exist. You decided, "They must be at fault!" That decision can move quickly into a downward spiral. We begin to look for experiences to confirm our beliefs that we're stuck, and of course, we find them. Even if they're not real examples, we'll twist and change the story so that it fits our narrative.

When information is missing in a story, it's easy to fill the missing parts with a narrative, which is typically negative and certain to confirm our own bias. For example, your partner was supposed to be home at seven o'clock for dinner, and now it's eight thirty and they're still not home. This may have happened several times and you feel disrespected, not important. You begin to imagine your partner's not paying attention to the time and that they're having fun at work or with someone else with no regard for your dinner plans. You may wind yourself up into a tizzy and become very upset: you can vividly picture your partner doing this to you; you haven't heard from your partner, you have no idea where they are, but you've created a full story surrounding their lateness. Then your partner comes home and you let them have it. The situation escalates into a fight where no one's happy. You find out later the story you concocted in your head was inaccurate and they actually had a flat tire, forgot their cell phone, and were miserable, just wanting to come home to you. Unfortunately, upon their arrival, you created a firestorm.

Although creating this narrative is our way of protecting ourselves, it may bring about really bad situations. Furthermore, it's unfair to those we attack. Since we have a choice as to the narrative we create, choose a neutral story to fill the gap of missing information. If we're unaware of what we're doing, we'll continue to craft stories to fill in missing information and keep ourselves in a victim state.

I've heard of research in this area where, when we feel like a victim or we feel stuck, our brains start to limit our problem-solving ability. So physiologically, we spiral down and become more "stuck" unless we have a tactic to help us when we find ourselves in these situations.

Tool Tips

A tool to use when emotions are high and a negative reaction to a situation is imminent is to "Take Ten." That means digest what happened for at least ten minutes, if not more. Try to remove the emotion from it, and try to see the other person's perspective and why they made the decisions they did. When you're ready to address the situation, be sure you can do so without heavy emotion attached. If you need more than a ten-minute time out, and if seeing the other person's perspective is tough, then follow the steps below.

View the situation. Recall it with as much accuracy as possible: What just happened? (Imagine you had to accurately document all sides involved.) How did you react?

Assess the meaning. What is the real significance now? Is there a need to follow up? If so, what outcome am I trying to achieve? (Do I want to rip the person apart or have them learn from the experience?) Pay close attention to your motivation as that will help direct the results you achieve.

Become curious. Why did the people react the way they did? Start asking good questions—not leading, judgmental ones. This takes you out of the seat of accusation and puts you in a place of being open to hearing what really took place.

Bring it to conclusion. What will you do now to create the best outcome, acting with grace and respect? Even if you disagree with the other party, you can be respectful. If you were to achieve the desired result, what actions would you need to take to get there?

If you follow these steps, you'll achieve greater success when those less-than-desirable moments happen. If all else fails, obtain an honest perspective from a person you trust.

Unleash Your Power

Kirsten Blakemore

Life, of course, happens at work and at home. How we react in each situation determines whether the outcome is favorable. While battles in business are common, challenges arise that are unique to women, and I strongly believe we must be supportive of one another. Tearing each other down at every opportunity to move ourselves ahead of others is counterproductive. The old folk adage seems to be true: what goes around comes around. What you send out is what you'll receive in return. Throughout my career, I worked with great people, and I worked with people who haven't found their own inner moral compass. The women who have stabbed me in the back hurt me more than have the men. Recently, I was working with a colleague, and I thought we were on the same page, connected with a similar vision. While attending a small business meeting, her words betrayed her, and her true agenda became apparent. I was dumbfounded since we'd just been talking about our shared vision. I thought we were aligned. In the meeting, however, she steered the conversation in a direction that was not in support of our previous conversations. It was a mouth-dropping moment.

Women need to support, mentor, and be truthful with other women. This doesn't mean that we need to blindly agree with everything every woman says. (At this point, I'm not addressing our interactions with men.) On the contrary, there has to be a code that we act with integrity with all women with whom we work, regardless of hierarchy. To achieve that, we must have a level of honesty and a willingness to be candid with one another, which likely requires discussions by which we achieve this, as we can't assume it. If we enacted this code in every organization, women would flourish. We'd have one another to lean on when things got tough. We'd be able to ask the tough questions and trust we were going to hear the truth. We'd be able to grow to the next level of development because there would be a foundation of trust. We could hear the hard things about ourselves and work through them.

This effort requires tremendous courage and a willingness to be vulnerable. I call it The Wonder Women code (TWW). Start it at your organization. Train the women about this code to be genuine with one another so that you can each develop and grow to your fullest potential.

One element of TWW code is to develop a coaching or mentoring program at your organization. Work with your human resources department or a manager and tell them you would like to develop and grow as an employee and that enacting this code would be a way to do that. You can follow this recommended format to provide a coaching program within your organization.

Start with two forty-five-minute sessions a month with a coach in the organization. (Ideally, the coach has been trained and certified.) Clearly define the parameters of the coaching program and any concerns, such as confidentiality. Determine that it's designed to be a developmental tool.

As an employee, define what you want to gain from coaching, and be up front about what you expect from your coach. "I'd like you to be brutally honest with me." Or if you're a bit more sensitive, tell them, "What I need from you is to be sensitive and honest but creatively gentle if you're telling me a tough truth."

Set the goal of the session. "In this session, I'd like to address this topic, and by the end of the session, I'd like to have this outcome/answer."

Practice curiosity. Coaches needs to be asking questions that make you consider alternative perspectives.

End the session by addressing whether you achieved your desired outcome for the session. In this manner, you'll have bookended the outcome. Thus, at the beginning of the session, you'll say what you hope to achieve, and at the end you'll address that outcome to determine if you achieved it or if it requires another session to explore it further.

The tools in this chapter also assist with the communication difference between men and women. Although not specifically addressing those gender differences, these tools will help you to be a better communicator.

Reflection:

Unleash Your Power

Kirsten Blakemore

Takeaway: We tend to fill in gaps of missing information with our own story, which is typically negative.

Fill the gaps with facts before fiction.

Your environment—people, situations—are indicators of obstacles that may be perceived or real. Use these indicators to define your potential next steps.

Be the driver of your journey, not the backseat passenger.

Journal: What is my environment telling me about how people see me?

Are people holding perceptions about me that may be working against me?

What actions can I take to move closer to creating alignment with my goals?

If there are situations at work in strife, go back to the first step: Define: what outcome do I hope to achieve in that situation? Then Align: what do I need to do to create that outcome?

Chapter 8: Wake Up Your Life!

"Every choice starts with a decision. Every decision starts with a thought. Every thought starts with a pre-conceived idea. It is up to you to decide what you do with each but always remember that the choice you make will result in the consequence you face."

Kemi Sogunle

Conscious Balance

Before I propose my approach to balance, let me preface it with this: In business, we're supposed to show up as our professional selves. In relationships, we're supposed to leave our business at the office. In physical and mental health, we're supposed to deal with these ailments by going to the doctor and taking a pill (or two or three). We segment off pieces of who we are and expect to be just a portion of a person. Stuff those other parts of you until you get home.

I've seen people who suffer from illness come to work and hide what they're experiencing. I myself have gone to work with cancer while going through a divorce simultaneously; I hid my pain. I thought if "they" knew, they'd exclude me from work, so I hid—as others have before me and likely will after. Maybe you can relate. I have a strong belief that a feeling of being overwhelmed, as well as anxiety and maybe even depression are more common/prevalent due to the fact we have to spend so much energy hiding who we are.

And so, balance. Everything we do and everything we are and have experienced make us unique with our own wisdom and perspective. Balance is out of whack when we have to focus on pretending to be something or someone we're not. Balance is out of whack when we show up to work pretending we don't have feelings or that we have to be "nice" to everyone because it's expected but not deserved. I believe balance is turned upside down when we stay in an unhealthy relationship. We do this because we have a warped belief that to stay in an unhealthy, unfixable marriage prevents our children from being hurt. We pretend, we hide, we manage, but inside, many of us are crying and feel so completely alone. There's no balance on that path.

What if it became common practice—not just common sense—to "be me," to be who we are all the time without apology? What if we just accepted every part of what makes us unique and ugly and beautiful? What if we could just release the shame, guilt, embarrassment, and perfectionist standards to accept and love who we are as we would our child?

All the energy we used to spend hiding, we'd now have for innovation. All the energy we used to spend fearing exposure, we could put into creating the life we've always wanted, living our "why." All the energy we used to

Kirsten Blakemore

spend fighting to defend our worth and value, we'd put toward greatness. Imagine it ... we would be awake and living a fully conscious, balanced life. At seventy-nine years of age, my mom has balance. She eats well, she has a healthy weight, and she takes no medication because she has no ailments. She exercises, meditates, and prays every morning. She's dealt with the experiences in life that have caused her pain, and she's forgiven those who hurt her. She holds no resentment, nor does she hide who she is. Drama comes into her life via other people, but she can allow it to pass like the wind. My hope is that I don't have to wait until I'm seventy-nine to have conscious balance.

Warrior Women

Women are complex, superhuman beings who multitask, nurture, strategize, create, love, solve, mentor, provide, and so much more ... on a good day. On a bad day, we can throw some (or all) of those qualities into the closet, say "to hell with it," and fight, compete, and be cutthroat. The key is to embrace all parts, not just the pretty ones.

Think of it this way: One day, when you leave the house, you know that at some point you'll meet Henry Cavil or Charlize Theron. Do you decide to leave the house in your flannel pajamas, mouthguard on, no makeup, your hair a mess, and say, "Honey, come here!" Likely not. We'd much rather be

Unleash Your Power

Kirsten Blakemore

dressed to the T, waxed, and coiffed as completely as possible, with the wind slightly blowing our hair back and music playing in the background. That's symbolically how many of us try to go to work or relate in our partnerships. We want to be all put together for presentation to our world. However, we may not have dealt with all our emotional issues from childhood, or the dysfunction in our family, or the current shame we feel. Sadly, though it remains unacknowledged, everything leaks out onto the world around us. Furthermore, we load our bodies with fast food and give up on exercise, only to wonder why our bodies are revolting against us with disease. And when we meet with conflicts because we haven't taken care of ourselves holistically, we can overreact. Feeling ashamed of our behavior causes the cycle to repeat.

Physically and chemically our bodies can work with us or seemingly against us. What are the ramifications to our body and mind when we're out of whack? When we're completely out of balance, we're more reactive, less patient, and have less control over our behavior. The state of imbalance doesn't help our brand at work or with our relationships.

Our daily life is filled with conscious and unconscious choices. When we thoughtlessly compartmentalize our life (into any of these parts—work, relationships, and health/wellness), we ignore parts of who we are. It's as though we're asleep at the wheel. If we ignore any portion of ourselves,

Unleash Your Power

Kirsten Blakemore

we're less in control of how we think and act and are more likely to inadvertently say or do something we regret.

For example, we've been multitasking our to-do list at home and still have to buy food for dinner. We rush through the process and end up yelling at someone who cuts in front of us in the grocery store line. An alternative choice would be to let the person step in front of us.

At work you have so many projects due, you struggle to keep your head above water. As you sit in your office trying to complete one of the tasks on your list, interruption after interruption invades your office. You're torn between having to pick up your kids and completing your tasks. When your direct report knocks on your door to ask for help, you explode and they rush out the door. (Oh … and now you remember you forgot to eat all day.)

We are warrior women attempting to complete everything in our lives at 100 percent. Of course, in the process we sometimes suffer from the demands we make on ourselves. We have at least three major areas that need attention, that require some nurturing, for us to find moments of conscious balance.

We must take care of our bodies, our health. This includes what we eat and drink, as well as the spiritual practice we have to nurture our soul. Exercise

keeps our stress levels down and our hearts healthy. Our bodies are our
sacred home. We have to treat them as such.

If we seek to be a professional, we must nurture our strengths and embrace
those areas where we need attention.

In our relationships (as a mother, friend, sister, wife), we must nurture our
self as well as those we love. We must be present with those people who
require energy and focus. So when the ship starts to tip, we're aware and
taking steps to right it.

Life moves extremely fast (except for those times during which we feel
badly when it seems to slow way down). If the tendency is to complete the
task list, we can miss making conscious choices. I call this sleepwalking
through life, sometimes just to get by. But as women, when we wake up our
life and create the life we've always wanted, watch out! This world will be a
better place when all women wake up to make conscious choices in all areas
of their lives, putting their best self forward instead of sitting in the corner.

Healthy Mind and Body

The saying "You are what you eat" makes sense. What we feed our bodies
determines how effectively they run. It's not reasonable to strive for
perfection when it comes to eating, but it makes sense to be mindful and
consciously choose the food we eat. Know your body and what foods make
it operate optimally and which foods do not. I can't eat a candy bar or

Kirsten Blakemore

doughnut in the morning without feeling physically awful. I may get a quick sugar high, but then I want to fall asleep.

Our food choices impact us emotionally as well as physically, both of which are important as we look for balance. We can choose to eat at Burger King frequently and then complain of being overweight. (Of course, our weight isn't at fault, or is it?) If we eat fast food and then feel shame or guilt about our choice, was it really worth it? Would you feel better emotionally if you chose something healthier? After years of weight and emotional swings relative to food, I decided to choose my food wisely, which doesn't mean deprivation. If I choose to eat pie, then I won't feel guilty afterwards. I just don't do that to myself anymore (most of the time anyway). The guilt and shame we put on ourselves directly related to body image damage our state of being.

This is why mindful eating is so important. Unconscious eating impacts our overall health and balance. When you make conscious choices about your food, those unwanted, self-deprecating emotions are less likely to come into play. When we experience shame, guilt, sadness, or anger, it can ooze out onto family members or workmates or both. Without supporting our bodies by eating well, exercising, and using some form of meditation or journaling for self-discovery, we're more reactive.

Kirsten Blakemore

Stress adds fuel to the reactive equation as well and increases cortisol levels, leading to a fight-or-flight mode. So physiologically, when we're stressed, our emotions are heightened. It's easier to fly off the handle.

Stress, fast food, and lack of sleep and exercise are an invitation for disease to find its home in your body. Some people are sensitive and feel the effects of stress on their bodies immediately; while for others it may take a while. The effects of stress can take the form of high blood pressure or high cholesterol. The pharmaceutical industry thrives because many of us go through life taking pills to solve our problems. It's estimated we'll spend $1.5 trillion globally on pharmaceutical drugs each year by 2021. When life speeds up, we can eat what's easily available, skip the exercise, and allow no time for introspection and meditation.

Notice which foods energize you and which make you feel poorly (whether physically or emotionally). Making conscious choices about your food and how often you exercise is important to your overall well-being and balance. Finding balance when it comes to your health is so important, and yet there's no cookie-cutter approach to achieving it because balance depends on you. There are factors that you can include or exclude from your life to support your everyday quest for balance, but it's personal. Some factors that are proven to influence the brain's ability to cope with stress are whether you eat properly, exercise daily, and provide your body with adequate sleep—all of which are so much easier said than done.

Here's the rub: When we're so busy, it's tempting (and easy) to make poor choices. Prepare, think ahead, and support yourself so that you're making good choices for your future.

Many gurus recommend meditation for a healthier mind because it aids our ability to improve self-awareness. The following are tips and tools to create the best outcome for your personal meditation.

Meditation apps like Calm or The Tapping Solutions allow for a ten- to fifteen-minute (or as long as you desire) mindfulness break. These breaks help you stay centered when things go off-kilter.

Be silent for five minutes every morning and when you go to bed. Clear your mind. Then set your mind as you would a clock. Appreciate what's good in your life, that for which you're grateful. This is called intentional discipline.

Focus on those aspects you want to increase. If you want to be rich, appreciate all the bills you've been able to pay this month rather than focusing on the deficit. Thank yourself for all the work you do to earn your paycheck so that you can pay those bills. That may seem silly, but you're focusing your mind into gratefulness. This is the way to achieve what you value and what you want to increase.

Unleash Your Power

Kirsten Blakemore

A calm mind supports being balanced. When we have this frame of mind, we're less likely to be impatient and critical. A grateful mindset improves our flexibility: we're less likely to be intolerant of people and situations when we have a happy, grateful frame of mind. When we lose that peace of mind, we open ourselves to impatience, intolerance, anger, disappointment, and feeling overwhelmed. Trust me, this isn't fertile ground for balance!

Professional Balance

Take a minute to think about how you show up at work. Are you leading and influencing others as your best self? In working with organizations for many years, I've witnessed strong leaders and dysfunctional ones. Strong leaders seek to improve themselves and are humble enough to embrace those areas in which they need to improve. There's a level of transparency and integrity that sets them above others. They embody courage.

However, consider this: We all grow up in families with some level of dysfunction. Maybe we're yellers, or when we communicate, we don't tell the truth, manipulating others to get our point across. Maybe one parent is the dictator and everyone else cowers. So many family dynamics are at play when we're young.

Now, imagine repeating that behavior over and over again until it's fully ingrained in us by the time we reach adulthood. Unless we're very aware or have had therapy to work through our family dynamics, they'll dictate our

interpersonal patterns. That means our organizations are filled with
hundreds of different family dysfunctions that haven't yet been processed
and replaced with more effective behaviors.

As adults, we bring to work both effective and not-so-effective relational
behaviors. Fear is one behavior I see frequently. The fear of the unknown
leads to a resistance to change. Fear can also be found in a resistance to
open, honest communication. It may be a fear of hurting people's feelings,
retaliation, or being excluded.

When speaking with groups within organizations, I frequently hear, "We
have a nice culture." There's a value to being nice to others, but the cost is
truth. The definition I've created regarding "nice" behavior is: "I'll be nice
to you, but in return, I expect you to give me what I want. If you don't, I'll
be passive-aggressive and show you that's not how the game's played."
Women are often expected to be "nice," and if we aren't, we're labeled as a
bitch. I was speaking with a group of high-performing women who pleaded
with me to unveil the secret to standing in their strength while not being
seen as a bitch. Unfortunately, it's a cultural belief we have to buck.

When we use our energy in the pursuit of pretending and hiding what we
really think, we don't have energy for other, more effective ways of thinking
and acting. If unchecked and unconscious, all of these dynamics cause us to
overreact, to say things we regret. Balance is showing up fearlessly in

support of self and others in a respectful way. Balance is being the authentic woman you are, your best self.

Relationships

Women, in superhero form, try to accomplish everything, and I've recently met more and more women who are the breadwinners, whose husbands stay home to run the household. They love what they do, they fulfill their "why," and their husbands love their role. Whatever position you're in as a friend, mother, sister, lover, and/or wife, you're likely juggling priorities. That feeling of being overwhelmed can set in quickly if we're not keenly aware of its approach. Understanding how you cope with being overwhelmed demands self-reflection. For example, perhaps to release anxiety, you clean or shop.

For years, I was in a very unhealthy marriage from which I had to emotionally disengage to survive. When I realized what I was doing, I knew my marriage would have to end. I didn't understand the impact that disengaging had on him until later, but I know that when life gets hard, that's my coping skill. What's yours? Having this awareness allows you the space to accept and embrace who you are, and to hold healthy boundaries so you can have moments of balance.

Choice

Unleash Your Power

Kirsten Blakemore

Ultimately, the way we treat our bodies, the foods we eat, the way we interact at work and in relationships, the stress we allow to negatively affect us, and our emotional state will influence our chance of disease, but we have a choice. Sometimes it doesn't feel like we do, but we choose how to respond to the people and situations in our life. We choose the food we eat. We choose how to care for our bodies and our minds. We choose to emotionally overreact or take a breath and pause.

The question is whether we prioritize self-love and compassion. Are those two nurturing attributes at the bottom of our list, or do we make them a part of our daily routine? Our decisions result in our effective or ineffective ability to cope with work and our relationships, ultimately impacting those around us. So when we feel stuck, like a victim, and we give in to that feeling, it affects not only our state of being but that of those closest to us. We're all connected to one another on this planet, and how we treat ourselves and others matters. We do have a choice to wake up and create a conscious life. First, we define, then we align with our desires.

Reflection:

Takeaway: You're a whole woman everywhere you go.

Stop hiding who you are; instead, use that energy to create your desired life. Wake up your life and make conscious choices to empower the working, relatable, healthy woman.

Unleash Your Power

Kirsten Blakemore

We create a healthy, balanced lifestyle—or not—based on our choices.

Use tools such as the Calm app or The Tapping Solutions app to support quick, mindful moments throughout the day.

Balanced nutritional choices and physical activity produce optimum health.

Unprocessed experiences from childhood can leak out when we least expect it.

Mindfulness is a choice. Incorporate some type of quiet time to process the day. Self-awareness is needed globally.

Journal: Are there any places or relationships in my life where I hide who I am?

What tools can I utilize throughout the day to support balance in my life?

Have I made choices recently that have betrayed my peace of mind?

What could I do differently in those situations to create a better outcome?

On a scale from 1-10, where am I now relative to balance (10 being complete balance, 1 being completely out of balance)? What would make me a 5? What would make me a 10?

Chapter 9: Design: Act with Courage, Faith, and Trust

"Rejection is merely a redirection; a course correction to your destiny."

Bryant H. McGill

Design

This is the final step in creating your desired outcomes for your life. To work this process, reflecting on what you've accomplished thus far is helpful and can be insightful, so I encourage you to document your progress. The Design step requires you to focus on what you need to do to continue your journey, no matter where you are. You may find you'll need to modify your goal due to unforeseen circumstances, so find your flexibility as you approach completion.

Have the chutzpah to keep going, even if you can't see the finish line— that's courage. Act as though you've already achieved the outcome you desire—that's confidence. Then keep going—that's consistency.

Courage

Recently I watched Reese Witherspoon (in her Netflix series Shine On with Reese) interview Dolly Parton. When describing her success and what it took to get there, Dolly recalled a story of her early years in Nashville. She came from a large, poor family and moved to Nashville when she was

Unleash Your Power

Kirsten Blakemore

eighteen to establish her talent as a songwriter and a solo artist, founding her own publishing company to maintain the rights to her music.

One of the early songs she wrote was "I Will Always Love You." Elvis Presley was coming to town to record his music and wanted to include her song. She thought, "How amazing! I'm going to meet Elvis and he's going to sing my song!" The day before he was to sing it, his people informed her that he had to have the publishing rights to her song. She said "no" to Elvis and was heartbroken when she learned he wouldn't sing her song without owning it. She cried that night, but she stuck to her guns and kept her copyright.

Years later, Whitney Houston sang that song, and Dolly felt proud of how the song sounded through Whitney's interpretation. Dolly's courage to stand her ground was what made that possible. What do you need in your life to support your goals?

Over the years as a coach and a speaker, I've asked women in executive positions to what do they attribute their success? Their answers included good coaches, mentors, trusted friends, and great teams, but what struck me was an overwhelming theme of authenticity and humility. They said they were willing to be wrong to get it right. They continued to ask and were open to learning. They did the right thing, even if their knees were shaking. This is courage—to be wrong to ensure you achieve the best outcome. Do

Unleash Your Power

Kirsten Blakemore

you have strong women in your life to whom you can turn, who will be honest with you? Will they tell you when they think you have it wrong? Do you have the courage to listen?

Courage is a prerequisite to achieving your desired life, just as it was with Dolly Parton. Courage propelled her to continue with her dreams. To have courage, one must deal with fear—fear of change and the unknown. Fear is often an obstacle to our forward movement. Whatever the reason for the fear, if desire causes us to forge forward, then we need courage to propel us. Self-doubt takes a toll and can easily derail you from keeping the course. Bryant McGill's quote from the beginning of this chapter ("Rejection is merely a redirection …") speaks to course correcting. Rather than seeing rejection as a negative or as something capable of robbing you of your dream, accept it merely as a course correction. That's a powerful interpretation because it assumes courage. With this mindset, you find some interesting turns along the way that you didn't anticipate.

Think of an airplane flying from Los Angeles to New York. It doesn't fly a straight path; it takes a curved route, flying where the traffic and weather are the least likely to interfere. When our course takes an unexpected turn, we need to roll with it and refuse to be discouraged. This is when we need courage. When our course takes that unanticipated turn and we're questioning the direction, many people give up, but it's exactly at this point that you need courage to continue to journey toward your goal. Use it as a learning moment.

Courage and faith are the traits required at this stage. Courage enables you to imagine and dream and really feel it's going to happen. You must believe, even when your negative talk can try to hold you back. Are your family and friends supporting you and your dream?

In the movies, we love the hero who demonstrates unbelievable courage against all odds. We especially appreciate the hero who continues the quest, even though she could potentially lose everything she values. The greater the risk, the more we love the hero for doing what's right. Why? Because we know how painstakingly hard it is to do what's right when many would take the easy path. There's always the character that tells the hero, "No one would fault you for walking away," yet we root for them to continue their pursuit, living vicariously through them, hoping beyond all hope that they triumph.

This is the faith required to walk into the unknown, onto the uncertain path. You'll hear the nagging doubts, yet you must continue anyway. Faith is required to continue with hope and a good attitude where you believe you'll achieve what you set out to do: believe you'll achieve!

I find my social media accounts help keep me focused on my goals. Because the majority of people with whom I'm connected provide motivational quotes or stories, those help me stay focused on my dream. I also have a "Happy" folder in my email box that contains messages from past clients who have thanked me, quotes that have really touched me, and stories to motivate me. I look at this folder when I need support.

I also surround myself with people who are working to achieve their dreams, so we support each other. It's easy to get sucked into those relationships at work that are gossipy and focused on drama or negative stories, but those won't help you move forward. Stay focused on what you want to achieve. Water what you want to grow. If you want more drama and negativity in your life, then continue to hang out at the water cooler and gossip. But if you're interested in making a change, achieving what you've not yet achieved, then find new people with whom to surround yourself.

It takes self-reflection and courage to be transparent. Relating with people without having hidden agendas is a critical part of building trust in a relationship. Associate with people you can trust and who are trustworthy. Search for the win-win in your relationships. You may experience fear when being transparent because it requires a level of vulnerability, but if your friends are trustworthy, they'll provide the space for you to be vulnerable without judgment.

Disappointments and Failures

Unleash Your Power

Kirsten Blakemore

I love this quote from Winston Churchill: "Success is the ability to go from one failure to another with no loss of enthusiasm." I would also call that "courage"…

Garth Brooks has a song that's impacted my life many times called "Unanswered Prayers." There is a line in the song that says, "Some of God's greatest gifts are unanswered prayers." Think back on your life. Perhaps you had a crush in high school, and you so desperately thought you wanted to date that person—maybe you even prayed you could date them—but it never happened. Then you go back to your twentieth high school reunion and you see that person's unattractive and holds absolutely no interest for you now. At this point, you'd think, Thank God for the unanswered prayer. We can't always catch a glimpse of why something didn't go our way, but a level of trust and willingness is required to learn in these circumstances.

If you interviewed for a job that you didn't get, trust that it wasn't the right one for you and then do your due diligence. Ask questions of the interviewer: "What could I have done better or differently in the interview? What was the deciding factor that ultimately led to your choice?" People rarely ask such questions, but they're so valuable to our development. Through questioning we learn and improve so that when the right opening occurs, we'll nail it.

Unleash Your Power

Kirsten Blakemore

We may not always get our desired outcomes when we want them or in the way we want them, but each circumstance is an opportunity for growth and improvement when you ask for feedback. When you do ask, simply listen, take notes, and then say, "Thank you." Take that information and inspect it; share it with a friend and ask their opinion. This information and feedback are gold, and it's how you continue to cultivate your brand. When disappointment happens—and it will—document it. What did you learn, where are your opportunities to improve, and where did you shine?

Lastly, when you encounter perceived failure, you have a choice as to how you'll react in the situation. Your choice is to assume the worst or assume the best. Many times we're faced with situations where we're not given all the information. For example, if you weren't given the job or promotion, the tendency is to fill that gap of missing information with a narrative, which is typically negative. You might say, "I don't know why I didn't get the job. Another candidate must have been better than I." We assume the worst, and sometimes we become so good at it that we may even create a story around it: "I really bombed the interview. They must have found a candidate who was really clever and nailed the interview. They probably had lunch together and connected, laughed it up. And I struggled. I could never be as good as that candidate."

Unleash Your Power

Kirsten Blakemore

In the same situation, we could choose a good narrative to fill in the missing blanks: "I didn't get the job. I'm going to ask for feedback in an email to find out what I could have done better. Next time, I'll be prepared with a story that demonstrates how I overcame obstacles to show my perseverance. This experience makes me better for when the perfect job does come along. I'll nail that interview and land the job I really want." Look at it as life's course correction.

This is when you need both courage and discipline. It's not always easy to stay positive when your course is corrected, but you can set yourself up for success by having an activity to support a positive mindset when events don't go as planned. For example, I'll call my friend who already knows what to say when I lose courage because I've prepped her ahead of time so she knows what I need to hear. Or I go on a long walk and clear my head, listening to music. Or I cook a new recipe I've been wanting to try. What would help you keep a positive mindset? This approach allows you to continue the journey.

You're defined by how you handle yourself in the face of disappointment. It's easy to be positive when times are good, but the moment life goes awry, that's when the rubber meets the road. The way you think and react to a person or situation is key. Do you handle your perceived failures with

Unleash Your Power

Kirsten Blakemore

grace? You can be disappointed inside, but your words and actions demonstrate grace.

An excellent example of grace in challenging, unfair times is illustrated in the movie Hidden Figures. All three women meet obstacles that none had faced before and overcome, yet they handled themselves with grace and dignity in adversity. They always behaved respectfully with their supervisors because it was the right thing to do. They handled themselves with grace and dignity during the most frustrating times and stayed the course, ultimately pioneering the way for others. Imagine if they'd given up or yelled at their boss, calling them a "good for nothing" just to stick up for themselves. It was because of their grace, dignity, and perseverance that they reached their goals and ultimately improved technology.

Today, times are different. Today, women can ask how the project could be improved and learn from it. You can be disappointed, but your words and actions demonstrate grace. We live in a time where women need to stick up for themselves and ask for feedback when we don't understand and are receiving any level of criticism. Furthermore, building one another up supports us being even better. If you're receiving anything less, ask for feedback.

Reflection:

Takeaway: We need courage when the unknown is in front of us.

Unleash Your Power

Kirsten Blakemore

Transparency is a healthy form of authenticity.

We need self-reflection to lead from a place of strength. There are always deviations to our plan.

Course corrections are a part of life.

We have a choice as to how we approach change.

Our attitude will define future choices.

Journal: Where do I need courage most in my life now?

What would it look like if I moved forward with courage in this situation?

Is there an area in my life that requires my attention that I've been ignoring? Where?

Do I handle perceived failures with grace?

Have I recently experienced a directional change that requires a shift in the way I view it?

Chapter 10: Confidence & Consistency

"You survived what you thought would kill you. Now straighten your crown and move forward like the queen you are."

Confidence is important when applying for a job, but even more important in order to be a strong leader. People will follow a confident leader. They're not so likely to follow someone who is openly riddled with self-doubt. If you feel as though you're lacking confidence, fake it till you make it. Continue like the leader and queen that you are. Some of us may not see that in ourselves, but it's time to find your value and move forward.

Much research has been done on confidence and competence. With regards to women, it's worth mentioning here because of the impact it has on us. Competence is an accumulation of skill, knowledge, and experience in a certain area. Confidence requires a belief in oneself, having self-trust and self-esteem. Research supports the idea that women need to feel fully competent in a skill before they'll feel confident. However, many men don't require a high level of competence to feel confident.

When there are open positions that require a certain skill set, men with low competence in this area but high confidence will pursue the position. On the other hand, women with high competence may see themselves as needing to further develop their skills and thus have low confidence, which means they won't pursue the position. Thus, more men acquire executive positions and leadership roles in the framework of competence and confidence, which can lead to men taking roles they weren't equipped to lead. (If this resonates with you, read The Confidence Code by Katty Kay and Claire Shipman.)

At what point can we accept our competence and move forward? Do we need to have a 60 percent competence level … 90 percent? According to the research, women's standards are much higher than men's. If we women need 80 percent competence before we feel we can apply for a specific role, men require much less of themselves at 30 percent. So the question remains: What will it take for us to embody self-confidence? When is enough, enough?

One step we can take is this: if you see a woman struggling with a lack of confidence, HELP HER! We're stronger together, and when we help each other, especially in this area, we're also helping ourselves. It's a win-win. The woman needing confidence gets a boost from your support, and you feel good for helping a struggling woman.

A friend of mine is an entrepreneur and just starting to work in a new area of business. Her current pricing model isn't appropriate for the new clients with whom she'll be working. As we were discussing her approach, she was struggling in one area: money. She felt very uncomfortable with her new pricing model. It was so much more than when she worked in nonprofit, but it was in line with what her competition was charging. The only

difference between them and her was that she hadn't built the confidence

around this increased pricing model.

As we continued to discuss it, she cringed, thinking about how she'd tell

this potential client about the cost, and yet many colleagues were telling her

that it was standard practice. She knew that she needed confidence in this

area and that creating the confidence to have these conversations was

integral to her ability to move forward. It didn't matter how many times I

told her she was worth it; she needed to change her belief system.

After many pep talks, role-playing, and strategizing how she would

approach money with this client, she had the conversation. She defined the

outcome of the conversation she desired, then she aligned her words to

create that outcome. She called me after her phone call with the client and

was absolutely ecstatic. She said the conversation went really well and the

client didn't push back on the price at all! She needed the confidence to

have the conversation, and in this case, "She faked it till she made it!"

Own It

One way to embody confidence is to own your current and past choices.

It's easy to own happiness, joy, and a feeling of fulfillment, but what about

when we're angry, resentful, and hurt? When we own our hurt as our

choice, we embody confidence. What would people do if one day we all

Kirsten Blakemore

decided to own and embrace all aspects of our being women and joyfully paraded around in our pajamas and mouthguards with our hair a mess. The world might not know what to do with us, but we'd be happy!

Learning from our mistakes helps guide us in the future. Years ago, I was miserable in a role I'd been hired to fill. I felt leadership was jerking me around, I didn't have support, and my boss was two-faced. I was ultimately asked to leave that role, which relieved me and made me happy.

When I think back to that position, I really didn't do what they asked me to because of other circumstances that arose. Instead of dealing with that head-on, I let it linger and dictate my moves. I now own my lack of leadership and direction in that position and the misery that I felt. Ultimately, I believe my misery came from the fact that I didn't feel equipped or supported to complete it. I felt like a victim. I should have owned that then so that I could have moved into a more empowered position of leadership, which I needed to succeed.

I learned a hard, valuable lesson. In retrospect, instead of holding a grudge against my boss, I should have owned my choices that resulted in an unwanted consequence. Because of this realization and because I now own the experience, I've changed my course in life and am now empowered to build up others. I'm controlling my destiny instead of ceding control to circumstances or another person. We create our future one choice at a time!

Unleash Your Power

Kirsten Blakemore

Sometimes we even have to generate our confidence in order to move forward.

We may encounter people who seem to be determined to prevent us from achieving our goals. When it becomes obvious to you, it's easy to fall prey to self-doubt and into the role of the victim. Your first response may be fear and anger, so simply acknowledge them so that you can move beyond them. Doing so enables you to decide on your next move from a place of centered choice.

Focus on the outcome you desire and work backwards. Decide what steps are required of you to get that desired outcome.

What doesn't kill us makes us stronger, and I feel like there are a lot of pretty strong women out there!

Consistency

All three steps—Define, Align, Design—require consistency. Even though your course may take some unexpected turns, don't give up. Instead, remember to follow these tips:

Redirect: Your course may change but keep your focus on the desired outcomes. There will always be deviations or, at the very least, surprises. Glue yourself to the goal.

Unleash Your Power

Kirsten Blakemore

Reframe: When you encounter something that appears to be an obstacle or a disappointment, you simply need to reframe it. Consider this example that happened to me.

Recently, I proposed an idea I wanted to have come to fruition at work. The team wasn't on board with my idea, and I could tell they wanted to move in a different direction. My initial reaction was disappointment, and I spent a few minutes discouraged because I was really passionate about this idea and wanted to see it birthed. I was concerned about one person who I thought was trying to sabotage it.

At that point, I recognized what I was doing to myself: I was creating a scenario of this person's intentional interference in my plan and starting to wind myself up. Fortunately, I caught myself and reframed my situation. I dug myself out of disappointment and positioned myself into a place of curiosity. Perhaps there's a better place for my idea to manifest itself—if not here, then somewhere else. I'm looking forward to seeing this happen and will look for opportunities to build it elsewhere. This is an example of reframing.

Resist: A temptation to quit may rear its ugly head. You may feel stuck when you can no longer see how you'll achieve your desired outcome. RESIST! Don't give up hope. Surround yourself with others who are optimistic. You can always find reasons or excuses for not reaching your goals. Instead, surround yourself with those people who energize you and your dreams, those who are also seeking ways to fulfill their goals and dreams.

Remembering these steps helps address a consistent attitude as well. Keeping positive is so helpful to having a mind that's open to new possibilities and new directions.

The second part of consistency is about you, your words, and your actions. Think about how you evaluate people and their performance. Typically, we judge people based on their words and actions, yet we judge ourselves based on our intentions. It's important that you focus on what you intend to do and then execute. If you say, "I don't like gossip" and then spend all your break time at the water cooler gossiping, people will neither know your intentions nor hear your words but instead see your actions. They'll judge you based on your actions and not on what you intended to do.

Just as athletes are judged on their consistency, so are we as professionals. If an athlete has an amazing game once in a while, they're not as valuable a player as one who is consistently able to perform. In the same way, if you meet your deadlines 40 percent of the time at work, it's likely that those around you won't have confidence in your word. If you want to be viewed as a valuable performer who honors your word, be consistent. Do what you say you'll do.

Unleash Your Power

Kirsten Blakemore

Being consistent seems so simple, yet when I'm working within organizations, I hear this as a common complaint. People have excuses for why they couldn't meet their original deadline. The bottom line is that we'll be judged on what we say we'll do and whether or not we do it. To be a valuable asset within your organization, honor your word and be consistent. People find comfort in knowing their colleagues will do what they say. Our friends feel the same, and this is how we build trust with one another. Thus, when something occurs unexpectedly, our knee-jerk reaction may be to get angry. Instead, it would be wise to remember the three steps: Redirect, Reframe, Resist.

Measure Success

One way of measuring success is to note the milestones we've completed or the major obstacles we've overcome. If an obstacle is more like a pebble on the path, you may not recognize the win, but even the small wins should be recognized and celebrated. How often do we simply continue to look to the next milestone in our journey and neglect to stop and celebrate the win? What's your measurement of fulfillment? A researcher said, "If you can't measure it, it doesn't exist." One way to track your progress is to reread your journals, look at your vision boards, and remind yourself of the affirmations you created. This is another reason why journaling is so important. Not only is it therapeutic and sets in stone what you want, but it also captures a specific moment on which we can reflect and determine where we've made progress. It's important to look back to the words written and the boards created because that's when you know you achieved what you set out to create.

When working with a new coaching client, I provide them with a series of questions to thoughtfully respond to and journal about. By the end of our coaching time together, we can reflect back on what was most important for them when we started and where they are currently on the journey. There's much to be learned when we document our thoughts, hopes, and dreams, when we have an opportunity to process and work on those and finally reflect on our progress. Responding to questions such as, "What would I do differently having gone through that?" and "What did I do really well that I want to repeat?" helps us take the time to measure our progress and recognize our efforts, which provides comfort, confidence, and fulfillment.

Fulfillment is a sense of achievement. No matter how small or large the task, when you accomplish it, you should feel fulfilled. As I work with groups, there's a tendency to focus on what needs to be accomplished and to overlook what was completed. I've yet to meet individuals and teams who feel they receive way too much recognition. Let's make this a priority.

Unleash Your Power

Kirsten Blakemore

Achievement of progress needs acknowledgement, which leads to the sense of fulfillment.

I think there's a false sense of how fulfillment feels. I can assure you that it doesn't involve trumpets sounding, balloons falling, and us living in the happy-ever-after. We may feel euphoric, but that's not a permanent state of being. I think fulfillment is achieved when we recognize what we've accomplished, moment by moment.

Look for evidence of the people, experiences, and events in your life who are supporting your dream. You may see something grab your attention on the Internet, or a friend may reach out with an opening that's the job of your dreams. Realize that dreams can continue to morph as you continue to desire new adventures. The sense of fulfillment is within you, and it simply requires you to tap into it daily.

The most important part of this equation of measurement is to celebrate the wins, no matter how small. Because life moves at a rapid pace, it's so easy to skip over those moments in which you realize you completed something important to you. Review your day to keep track in your journal, reread your journal to look for evidence of your accomplishments, and then celebrate. Recognize yourself and honor your efforts. Make the time to share your accomplishments with a friend who will support your efforts.

Finally, recognize those women in your life who can use appreciation. Let's build each other up. We can do so much more when we do it together!

Reflection:

Takeaway: What doesn't kill us makes us stronger.

Confidence is generated within; no one can give it to us.

Confidence and competence are intertwined.

If you see a woman needing confidence, help her.

Your path will change directions, but consistently keep your eye on the outcome.

Be a source of consistency so that people can depend on you.

Add value by honoring your word.

Rejection is simply a course correction.

One way to perceive success is to look at the obstacles you've overcome.

Recognize progress and celebrate the wins.

Journal: What experience has made me stronger?

What does it take to make me feel more confident?

Where in my life do I need confidence? What steps can I take to "fake it till I make it?"

Is there a situation that's recently occurred that I need to redirect, reframe, and/or resist?

Where are my consistencies? List my consistent attributes.

Unleash Your Power

Kirsten Blakemore

What is one thing for which I'm grateful that occurred this past week?

Today?

How would I define fulfillment? Now imagine I'd accomplished everything on that list. Can I experience that fulfillment as I imagine it?

Chapter 11: All for One and One for All

"Each time a woman stands up for herself, without knowing it possibly, without claiming it, she stands up for all women." Maya Angelou

I want to end this book with a message of hope, and with the possibility of what we can do to inspire hope for other women and ultimately change the balance in the world.

Little did Harvey Weinstein know that his criminal behavior would send a ripple effect throughout our culture, igniting women in a way like never before. His atrocities caused the sleeping beauties to awaken and unite, resulting in the #MeToo movement.

This ripple effect gave "Kate" the courage she needed to move forward with one of the boldest moves she's ever made in her life. Kate joined a private company which was founded by men with a strong similar background. Upon joining, she was told that, according to their beliefs, if a man and a woman were in the office alone as the day came to an end, one of them would need to leave as they believed it was not appropriate for men and women to be alone if they're not married. Another rule that must be obeyed was that the company not service organizations that sell vice products, such as tobacco or alcohol.

At first glance, everyone was so nice, and she was glad she'd joined the company. In time, however, she realized that her gender would stand in the way of success despite all her efforts. She tried many tactics to be invited to projects that would shape her development, experience, and salary, but none seemed to work. She asked for feedback on multiple occasions (even begged for it) and found ways to bring some of the men into her projects in the hope they would reciprocate, but the bias was too strong.

One of the founders said early on that women are just not as powerful as men and that men in business like to work with men. But it wasn't until she heard that the men, who joined the company at the same time she did (with lesser education), were offered almost twice as much in salary as she earned that she decided she needed to take a different approach.

She loved what she did but struggled with how to change the bias. It wasn't that they were mean people, but their beliefs were discriminatory. After several years of failed attempts to change the culture, news of the salary differential and the wave of women finding their voice created a perfect storm. Kate decided she would file a claim with the Equal Employment Opportunity Commission (EEOC) to see if she could create positive change and simultaneously continue to work the craft she loved.

After the claim was filed and the company notified, change began—slowly, but it was happening. The courage required to stay in an uncomfortable environment (in which many of the leaders would hear of her claim and could make it even more difficult for her) was unwavering. Little by little a leader would change his approach to be more inclusive—or maybe the change came from Kate.

Kate couldn't have done this and stayed employed if it weren't for the courage of so many women who were now in the public eye. The courage women are demonstrating today is causing a tidal wave of movement in the right direction for women: equity amongst genders.

And it's not just women like Kate. Women everywhere are standing up to their perpetrators for victimizing them when fear prevented this before. The largest sexual assault scandal in sports has finally concluded with gymnasts standing up to their perpetrator, Dr. Larry Nassar. Even court hearings are being handled differently as a result of women rising up.

In the case of the gymnastic sexual assault hearing, Judge Rosemarie Aquilina allowed any woman or girl abused by Nassar to testify in court as a way of healing her soul, and 156 women found their voices and shared their stories. During an interview, Judge Aquilina acknowledged she's been criticized for allowing the courtroom catharsis and ultimate justice. Her courage to support the women in the courtroom wouldn't have happened even twenty years ago. She's acting on behalf of those who could not and are now seeking justice. Her belief is that she's allowing women to heal from the impact of being molested. She's on a crusade to end sexual assault forever.

Unleash Your Power

Kirsten Blakemore

And that's not all. Today, we see more women standing up for themselves and for others than ever before. The US National Women's Soccer team went to court to demand equal pay, and it doesn't stop there! The Project is a voluntary challenge to increase women's presence as contributors and on-air journalists. (Typically journalism is heavily male dominated.) Simply by paying attention to the ratio, the diligence has paid off as 74 percent of teams devoted to the result reached a goal of 50 percent women contributors in April 2019, and more than 500 teams have signed up for the challenge. This is progress! Women, we are stronger together.

Sadly, when we focus on others, we tend to compare, judge, and become critical. In this age, diversity and inclusion are at the forefront of change within courageous organizations that desire to improve their culture. While embracing difference is more prevalent than ever before, we still have miles to travel. When we judge others and ourselves, we limit possibilities. We can no longer afford to be critical or judgmental but must stand strong and band together to make a difference.

After day one of a diversity and inclusion conference in San Francisco (a city I love), I sat with approximately twenty other women and men at a dinner in a downstairs private room (which felt like a cozy cave). The host, Fairygodboss, is a company devoted to elevating women in business. Alison Vorsatz, senior enterprise director, requested that we introduce ourselves, state who we are and who we work for, and "why" we're interested in spearheading the D&I effort. She also asked that we include "a brag."

As she kicked the introductions off, I was truly moved by her story as she set the tone for everyone else in the room to be equally vulnerable. She was at a crossroads in her business life and knew she wanted to be in service. She had a dream of quitting her job and going to Africa to help native girls in need. I was astonished by the tremendous vulnerability created amongst strangers, some of whom teared up when they stated their "why." While I was stunned, I was also so comforted.

We were all united by a cause: to better our company culture by creating an inclusive environment where people are treated fairly and have a sense of belonging. We desire a culture where difference is celebrated and where people at all levels of a corporation value all people, not just some.

After dinner I walked—actually skipped—back to my hotel room and lay in bed wondering if we'd ever experience a time when this feeling of inclusivity would realize itself in business. My mind was racing with all the possibilities that lay ahead, and I fell asleep with such a warm feeling, one of hope. The next morning, I was excited to experience day two at the conference and was blown away by the tremendous feelings of hope and possibility. We heard speaker after speaker describing their amazing work in the world.

Unleash Your Power

Kirsten Blakemore

One gentleman, Joe DeLoss, founder & CEO of Hot Chicken Takeover (he calls himself the Head Chicken Fryer), told us that he gives back to the world by hiring people with "alternative resumes"—people with a criminal record. Having a criminal record challenges any individual seeking employment, and of course, a job is necessary for rehabilitation into a community.

DeLoss shared that he's developed a business staffed with loyal employees because he truly cares about giving back to people who may have lost their way and are now trying to reclaim their lives. He's pushed through the irrelevant traditional business model and created his own to support his employees.

For example, instead of offering a 401(k), he offers other benefits that are more important to his talent pool, such as salary advances for a down payment on a new place to live. His mindset is "How can I serve not only fried chicken but also people?" In an industry with a high employee-turnover rate (150 percent according to), is incredibly low at 34 percent. This is only one example of what can happen when we're committed to being in service and creating an equal playing field for all.

We were mixed and moving around all day, meeting new people and engaging in innovative activities. Everyone was kind, hopeful, and just as eager to turn the feeling we were all having into a reality for everyone in their respective businesses. It felt amazing to be in a room of 500 people all committed to serving others, creating a sense of belonging at work and embracing our differences. Imagine if we could bottle this feeling and have every employee feel this good at work. How much more effective, innovative, and profitable would we be at work? Employee engagement would rise along with morale, turnover would decrease, and women would be commonly considered for executive positions.

Women are closer than ever before to equal opportunity, but we're NOT there—not by a longshot. We must continue to be diligent when choosing our workplace; we must select the right employer, one committed to hiring and promoting both women and men. According to McKinsey's ongoing research called , having a diverse executive team and/or board with female representation shows an increase in profitability. Many companies and online organizations are available to help women find the right organizations. With all this momentum, women will be represented in executive leadership roles.

As I mentioned before, Fairygodboss is the largest career community for women. Their mission is to improve the workplace for female professionals through greater transparency. Fairygodboss works with over 125 major US companies, helping them attract top female talent and enhance their employer brand among women. Employers can increase the number of qualified applicants to their open positions, share their story about why they're a great place for women to work, and engage their current workforce.

A critical trend occurring now is gender pay. We must demand equal pay for the role that offers the same value, regardless of the gender of who is performing it. is a consulting firm that spearheads this work with their clients, offering direction on how to even this playing field and then assess where employees are experiencing the change.

The news often carries stories about women who discover they've been underpaid for the same role as their male counterparts, but how do we know if we're being underpaid comparatively when a company isn't transparent? Most of the time we don't. According to the , a law was created (by a man?) that you must file an Equal Pay Act (EPA) claim/charge within two years for unlawful compensation (or three years if it's a willful violation). But if you don't know what others get paid, how can you file a charge within the allotted time? And what happens if you miss the window of opportunity to file?

Last year for my forty-ninth birthday present to myself, I attended Marianne Williamson's women's weekend event. The focus was to have women commune together for a weekend to learn and to share stories of love and forgiveness. I so desperately needed the weekend to nurture my feminine side, to heal. More than 300 women filled the LAX Marriott that weekend. There was learning time, quiet time, and time to connect.

As I was waiting for the second day of the program to begin after lunch, a woman next to me leaned over and introduced herself as Linda Lavin. We discussed our learnings and found an instant connection. We were both from Maine, grew up near each other, and had followed Marianne on and off for many years. We knew we had a bond that would outlast the end of the seminar and went to lunch the following week. As we shared, I mentioned I was writing a book for women and specifically my experiences around earning less than men in equal roles.

Linda shared with me that she recalled an episode of Alice, in which she starred, playing the lead role in the series that ran from 1976-1985. In this storyline, Mel hired a male waiter to do the same job that Alice, Flo, and Vera were doing, but he was offered more money. The women stuck together and quit the diner until Mel promised to make it right. This is a tune of inequity that has been playing way too long. It's time to break this record.

The culture fit not only has to do with equal pay for similar roles, however, but also the potential career path. Is there a defined career path? If not, do they invest in helping women learn, and will they mentor, sponsor, and develop women so that they're able to grow as employees as well as move into leadership and executive roles?

If you're an entrepreneur, there are companies devoted to empowering women to be successful. is a strategic communications firm focused on the growth and strong presence of women. Want to know what's happening in the world of women? Subscribe to , which is where I first heard of the BBC challenge.

As I end this chapter, I feel compelled to provide my "why." Twenty-six years ago, I entered into a marriage relationship that would turn into twenty-four years of what felt like prison. It was unhealthy, and I felt controlled, as though he were pressing down on me with his thumb. I couldn't be who I'm meant to be and stay in that relationship.

Four years ago I was diagnosed with melanoma. It took a cancer diagnosis for me to decide I'd no longer settle for less than who I am. I finally asked myself, "Will I die because I chose not to value myself—to stand up for me? Will I die because I literally was eating myself from the inside out? Will I die with my music left in me?"

It was the wake-up call I needed to break my lifelong pattern of not owning my worth as a woman, and I couldn't have had the courage without my mother by my side as she walked a similar path. Her love and support got me through the toughest moments in my life.

Unleash Your Power

Kirsten Blakemore

My "why" is that I stand for not only myself and my value, but also every other woman willing to stand for hers.

This chapter's focus is devoted to providing a strong case for change. We must make changes. No longer can we wait idly by for someone to give us a handout. We must wake up and create the life we've always wanted but were too afraid to choose. You're worth it! You deserve the life you desire. When doubt creeps in to your mind, remember to change the narrative playing out from "I can't" to "Why Can't I?"

Use the resources to help you as you move forward. Use the book to take the 3 Steps—Define, Align, Design—and the tips, tools, and guidance to develop, nurture and bring out the best YOU. We cannot assume that someone will give us a handout because we're female and therefore should wait to see what happens. No, we must focus on our results—the results we provide every day at work and home. It will require your commitment to the cause, and the cause is ripe. Women will rise up, unite together, have each other's backs, and receive the equity that's rightfully ours.

Conclusion: Live it!

The contents of this book are intended to arm you with a system to achieve your goals, lead from a place of authenticity, and strengthen your relationships through self-awareness. The methodology is using these three steps: Define, Align, Design. Within each step is a myriad of suggestions designed to help you clearly articulate what you want and to reflect on those goals.

You can use this process for small goals. For example, imagine an exchange leads you into an argument with someone that leaves you both bothered, hurt, and wondering what to do. At that moment, define the outcome you want, and align your thoughts, words, and actions to achieve that outcome. Design as you speak with that person to settle the conflict. Remember, a course correction may be required.

The method is also ideal for big dreams and goals. The process provides the clarity of outcome and the feelings associated with achieving the goal. Follow the steps in the Align section to ensure you're actively supporting your vision. Design what it will look like. Know that likely you'll have many course corrections along the way. Find your strength group—true friends, reading, "journaling"—to support you staying the course, and continue to build your path. Celebrate the small steps as well as the large ones.

Kirsten Blakemore

Consider this illustration of the application process: it's like a sprint versus a marathon. In an argument, you'll need to apply the process quickly and diligently, with continuous self-awareness and ongoing reflection until you reach the outcome. For a bigger goal, such as becoming a CEO, it's more like running a marathon. You need a steady pace, with specific mile markers laid out along the journey.

Think about all the people in businesses who move through a day with little self-reflection and awareness of their actions. Their actions or inactions have an impact on those around them. Ripple effects are created. How often do you spend reflecting on intentions, motivations, thoughts, and feelings? Look for evidence as you increase your self-reflection and awareness as it impacts others. Imagine what would happen if more people applied the three-step process of Define, Align, Design. Imagine the potential impact this would have within your company, relationships, and ultimately, your goals.

I want to finish Melissa's story that I introduced in the beginning of this book. You may recall that she felt overwhelmed and undervalued by her CEO, who was purported to be a bully. This was a man of impressive height and weight who had a loud, commanding voice and used sarcasm frequently in conversation. In fact, he knew that people considered him a bully.

Unleash Your Power

Kirsten Blakemore

I asked her to read an early draft of my book and spent time coaching her. Over a period of a few years, I witnessed his leadership style with her and others. I heard the stories of negative experiences he'd created by going over her head, demeaning her in front of others in meetings, and withholding information that was vital to doing her job effectively. She would be exhausted and feeling at her wit's end, yet something in her gut kept her there. We even talked about her defining her ideal role at her ideal company, but she continued in her job, always doing her best.

It would be easy for anyone on the outside looking at this example to determine what she "should" have done, but I heard her resolve on more than one occasion that she knew she needed to stay. In the beginning, she stayed for the people whom she helped. Every day people called her or came to her office for advice. Truly committed to helping people, she was fulfilling her purpose by helping people who were really, really struggling. At one point, an employee came to her who was giving up on life. The work and leadership struggle was too much for him to bear. She helped him through it, even calling him at home to make sure he was okay. At one point I asked her, "What about you helping yourself? What would that look like?" She felt fulfilled, however, knowing she positively impacted people daily.

Kirsten Blakemore

Through it all, though, she kept her eye on what it would look like to have the perfect role, a role she was defining in her head and on paper. She was able to recite to me attributes of both the job and the company that she would find ideal. She was committed to making a difference in a company that honored her worth and valued her as an employee. She wanted to ensure there was no glass ceiling built above her, and she wanted to utilize her talents and skills in a greater scope. Through this process she defined and redefined what she wanted.

She shared with me stories of how the CEO would cut her off at the knees. He'd use sarcasm to make a point, and it was biting and hurtful to her. She frequently apologized. In one coaching session I asked her, "Why are you apologizing?"

She had to think about it for a moment. Then she said, "I guess I'm apologizing to make him feel it's okay. But it's not okay."

She had an awareness in that moment that she frequently apologized, so she began to note every time she caught herself saying "I'm sorry" when it wasn't an apology. In our next session, she described how often she found herself saying this. She then made a commitment to align her thoughts and words around the goals she created for herself: for others to see her value and to work for someone who valued her. She learned to stop herself from apologizing before she uttered the words. This pattern was deeply rooted for her and making the shift in behavior required self-reflection and awareness to which she committed.

She started seeing changes in how people interacted with her, and she felt more empowered in the design of her life. Gradually, her work experiences started to shift. The new board solicited her help to assess the CEO, and after a long, laborious process in which she was a pivotal player, the CEO was asked to leave the company.

There were times during this extremely confidential process in which she thought she wouldn't be able to lead this charge. She had so much pressure on her with no way of expressing it to others. However, she's now in a very good position with a board that values her and what she offers. They see her moving into bigger roles, with more responsibility and challenges, which excite her. She's eagerly looking forward to her next steps.

Never forget you have value. It's up to you to be the best version of you. It's in there –bring it out for the world to see. Unleash Your Power!

Reflection:

Journal: Where can and will I use this three-step process?

What goals do I want to achieve now?

How will I begin?

When will I begin?

Who can I ask to hold me accountable to my dreams and my timelines?

Unleash Your Power

Kirsten Blakemore

About the Author

Kirsten Blakemore is an executive coach, speaker, and author who empowers women to

step into their full potential with confidence and authenticity. With years of experience

helping women in leadership and business, Kirsten brings a blend of practical strategies

and heartfelt wisdom to her work.

Her mission is to guide women to define their own success, align with their values, and

design lives they truly love.

Connect with Kirsten at:

www.kirstenblakemore.com

www.ingramcontent.com/pod-product-compliance
Lightning Source LLC
Chambersburg PA
CBHW071600040426
42452CB00008B/1242